Educational Reform with Television

THE EL SALVADOR EXPERIENCE

Educational Reform with Television

THE EL SALVADOR EXPERIENCE

John K. Mayo, Robert C. Hornik & Emile G. McAnany

Stanford University Press, Stanford, California 1976

Stanford University Press
Stanford, California
© 1976 by the Board of Trustees of the
Leland Stanford Junior University
Printed in the United States of America
ISBN 0-8047-0896-7   LC 75-7484

Preface

In recent years countries throughout the world have experienced an increasing demand for education and for a better quality of instruction at all levels. The need for a reevaluation and reform of school systems has become particularly acute in the developing countries of the Third World, which have traditionally used imported educational philosophies and techniques mostly to train relatively small, elite segments of their societies. Urged to make their systems more democratic and more responsive to genuine economic and social needs, Third World planners have attempted both to improve their populations' overall access to schooling and to enhance the quality of that schooling through curriculum reform and the incorporation of modern teaching methods. In the last decade communication technologies, and particularly television, have become increasingly important in such programs. Planners are more than ever aware of the mass media's potential usefulness—and especially of the possibility of transmitting high-quality instruction simultaneously throughout a school system. Critics of this trend point out that a reliance on the kinds of communication technologies now exported by the industrialized countries can only reinforce an already undesirable dependence on the cultures of those nations, making needed structural reforms in the Third World much more difficult.

Arguments over the proper role of communication technology in Third World education have raged for a number of years. In *The World Educational Crisis* (1968), Philip Coombs characterized as either "utopian" or "cataclysmic" the arguments for or against the expanded use of communication technology in education. The major problem has essentially been one of information: lacking sufficient evidence on the performance of existing educational broadcasting systems, proponents and critics alike have tended to hold rather rigid and largely rhetorical positions on the subject. With the emergence of El Salvador's instructional television project in 1968, however, a unique opportunity was presented to observe in detail the effects of introducing television to the school system of a developing country, and thus to move the debate to a more realistic plane.

El Salvador's experience with television is unique in many ways. Unlike other countries that have attempted to upgrade one or another aspect of their educational systems with television, El Salvador conceived of the medium as the cornerstone of a thoroughgoing reform. The comprehensive nature of that reform, which included curriculum revision, new methods of teacher training, and new concepts of school supervision and pupil evaluation, demanded a much broader basis of evaluation than that used to assess television projects in other countries. Accordingly, the authors and their colleagues in El Salvador and at Stanford University spent more than five years gathering and interpreting the data that is presented in this book.

In spite of the authors' close association with El Salvador and its educational system, the focus of this book extends beyond the borders of that fascinating country. In many ways, the Salvadorean experience can be viewed as a case study wherein the basic processes and problems underlying educational reform are discussed. The difficulties encountered by Salvadoreans in their efforts to use television effectively in the schools are in large measure the same problems other countries have faced and will continue to face as they try to effect basic changes in their educational systems.

The research reported in this volume would not have been possible without the help of many people. We are particularly grateful to Professor Wilbur Schramm, former director of the Institute for Communication Research at Stanford, who directed the research project. His unparalleled experience, good sense, and deep respect for El Salvador's reform project inspired us throughout the field study and the subsequent task of putting our results into book form. We are also indebted to Dr. Henry T. Ingle, who served as the last director of field research in El Salvador and initiated a number of innovative strategies for making the results of the study more useful to Salvadorean planners and administrators.

To our colleagues in El Salvador—Fernando Valero Iglesias, Ana María Merino de Manzano, German Rodríguez, María Ester de Zamora, José Ramiro Velasco, Victor Zelada, and Nohemy de Erhardt —we wish to express not only our thanks for a job well done, but also our enduring gratitude for the thoroughly professional and unselfish manner in which they gave of themselves during the many long and difficult phases of the study. We also thank the Agency for International Development and the Academy for Educational Development in Washington, D.C., whose financial and administrative support made the research possible, and whose officials were always respectful of our need for sufficient time and autonomy to get the job done.

The Ministry of Education freely provided us with information at all stages; and many of the photographs used in this book are from its files.

At Stanford, we are particularly grateful to Jim Trosper, who, in addition to making many useful editorial suggestions, was instrumental in transforming our final manuscript into book form. Ann Roberts, along with Liz and Greg Jones, also made major contributions to the preparation of the book.

In the course of the work in El Salvador, hundreds of teachers and students were asked to complete questionnaires, to take various tests, and to participate in various evaluation tasks. Without their cheerful tolerance and interest, often in the face of tedious demands and deadlines, the study would not have been possible. We also benefited from the encouragement and support of officials within all levels of the Ministry of Education. If in some small way this book helps to convey the richness and complexity of El Salvador's educational reform with television, it will have done so largely through the efforts of these people, whose experience and insights we were fortunate to share.

J.K.M. R.C.H. E.G.McA.

Contents

Tables and Illustrations

FIGURES

*Photographs of El Salvador's teachers, students, and ITV
system appear on pp. 32, 35-36, 47, 78, and 133-34.*

Educational Reform with Television

THE EL SALVADOR EXPERIENCE

Introduction

In January 1969 the young Salvadorean Oscar Miguel Ramírez was
about to enter the seventh grade. At fourteen, he had already acquired a great deal of practical experience working in his mother's
small grocery store, occasionally helping his father at the coffee
finca, and looking after his five younger brothers and sisters. Because
he was a conscientious student, Oscar's parents had high hopes for
him. His father foresaw the day when Oscar would be working at
the finca not as a picker but as a mechanic or an accountant in the
manager's office; his mother hoped her son might someday study at
the university to become a doctor. However, Oscar was regarded
somewhat suspiciously by many of his older relatives. No one in
the family had ever finished primary school, and the boy's accomplishments made them uneasy. They questioned the usefulness of so
much expensive schooling, and felt that it might make Oscar selfish
and ashamed of his humble background.

Oscar's hometown had not changed much during his lifetime.
Only the central plaza and a few surrounding streets were paved,
and in the dry season everything was covered with dust. Water and
electric power were erratic. Except for staple goods such as rice,
beans, candles, and soap, most townspeople preferred to travel by
bus to San Salvador, the capital city, for their weekly shopping. The
town had no movie theater, and for this reason Oscar and his friends
also liked to go to the capital whenever time and money permitted.
Very few of Oscar's schoolmates planned to stay in the village as

adults, since the opportunities and diversions of the big city were much more attractive.

The secondary school Oscar was about to enter was an adobe building rented by the government from private owners. It had six small classrooms, each with shuttered windows that let in little daylight and made the air incredibly stuffy during hot months. In each room the students' tables and benches were crowded from the back wall to within inches of the teacher's desk. On the wall behind the desk were a large blackboard, a religious picture, and a calendar distributed by one of the country's soft drink bottlers. Spread sparsely around the walls were portraits of Salvadorean heroes, a map of Central America, and a few student drawings. Aside from textbooks and a few pieces of scientific apparatus donated over the years by local patrons or left by former teachers, the school had very few learning aids.

Unlike Oscar's primary teachers, who lived in town and were well known to most residents, the secondary teachers commuted from the capital. Some came and went daily in a car pool; others arrived on Monday morning and stayed through Friday afternoon, boarding at local homes during the week. This was a life-style that many students would also have to adopt when and if they chose to continue their education beyond the ninth grade. Most of the teachers were young men who preferred city work; but, lacking seniority or political connections, they had ended up in the countryside. Despite some displeasure over this rural assignment, the teachers as a group were hardworking and friendly. They had all been raised in small towns and thus had considerable empathy for the young people they taught.

As the new term approached, Oscar looked forward anxiously to meeting his new teachers and classmates. Only half of his small sixth-grade class had decided to go on to secondary school; the rest were already picking coffee or looking for other kinds of work. Most of Oscar's new classmates, in fact, would come from neighboring towns. He was used to new faces, however, since he had already switched schools a number of times and had been forced to repeat the first grade when the director of his school decided he was not ready to advance. Had he not lost touch with his original school-mates, Oscar would probably have been surprised to learn that of the 40 students who began first grade with him, only four would ever enter seventh grade.

In 1968, Salvadorean newspapers began announcing that the government had launched an educational reform. Rumors spread that new schools would be built, that the curriculum would be changed, and that television would soon replace many teachers in the classroom. It was no wonder that Oscar was excited when he learned on registration day that his class would be one of the first to receive television. For the next three years, Oscar and a thousand like him would be part of a project designed to transform their country's educational system. How these young pioneers fared with television and the other elements of El Salvador's Educational Reform is the subject of this book.

Our study of El Salvador's instructional television system (ITV) was undertaken for three reasons: (1) to evaluate the effects of the new system on students, teachers, and school administrators, (2) to contribute data gained from this research to the future development of the ITV system itself; (3) to derive general conclusions that might help guide other nations interested in applying ITV or some other instructional technology. These objectives were translated into specific research plans that guided the collection of field data over four years.

To place the study of El Salvador's ITV system in proper historical perspective, Chapter One provides some basic facts and figures about the country, its economy, its educational system, and the development model pursued by its political leaders.

Previous studies of ITV have often overlooked a key determinant of success or failure by failing to examine the ability of a project's administrators to identify and solve problems. Accordingly, we compiled a general administrative history in order to shed light on the major decisions and problems that affected the development of the ITV system in El Salvador. The major conclusions of this effort are reviewed in Chapter Two.

A major goal of the ITV project in El Salvador was to improve the quality of student learning. Consequently, two kinds of learning were evaluated in the course of this study: basic skills (i.e. reasoning and reading ability) and course achievement. The actual learning performance of three successive generations (cohorts) of students was analyzed, and background information on the students, their schools, and their communities was also collected. Such information permitted us to see how students were affected by different environments and to determine what kinds of students achieved most with television and the other Reform programs. The results of these studies are presented in Chapter Three.

Measures of student attitudes toward ITV and school in general were repeated throughout the four years of research. Such measures provided a composite profile of a new generation of Salvadorean students, as well as useful background information with which to interpret their learning performance. This investigation is summarized in Chapter Four.

Because Salvadorean planners had conceived of the Educational Reform as a means to expand their country's supply of middle-level technicians, students' educational and occupational aspirations were monitored continuously. In addition, the career plans of the first group of ninth-grade graduates who had studied with television were examined in a special interview study. A second special interview study was undertaken to determine what educational and occupational hopes Salvadorean parents held for their children and how familiar the parents were with the schools, with ITV, and with the Educational Reform. The results of these studies are reported in Chapter Five.

Resistance to new educational technology among classroom teachers has been a contributing factor in the failure of a good many ambitious development projects. In El Salvador, therefore, we were very much concerned with teachers' attitudes toward ITV, toward the reforms that accompanied ITV, and toward the profession of teaching itself. In addition, a special classroom observation study was undertaken to determine whether classroom teaching methods were actually changing under the Reform. The results of these studies are reported in Chapter Six.

By eliminating tuition payments in grades one through nine, and by liberalizing enrollment and promotion policies, El Salvador's planners wished both to expand their school system and to make it more efficient. Archival and survey data were analyzed to see precisely how enrollment and efficiency were affected by these policies and to determine what their effects were on the unit costs of the ITV system. The results of these studies, along with a general cost analysis of the ITV system itself, appear in Chapter Seven.

Finally, Chapter Eight reviews the major accomplishments of El Salvador's ITV system, and raises some questions about its future and its relevance to similar projects in other countries.

CHAPTER ONE

The Setting

El Salvador is the smallest and most densely populated country on the American continents, occupying only 8,200 square miles. Bordered on the north and west by Guatemala and on the northeast by Honduras, it is also the only Central American nation that does not have an Atlantic coastline; however, its jagged Pacific coastline stretches for 160 miles.

The hot, humid climate that typifies the Central American isthmus prevails throughout El Salvador's coastal lowlands. Between sea level and 2,500 feet, where most Salvadoreans live, temperatures usually stay betwen 72° F and 81° F year-round; the higher interior regions of the country are somewhat cooler.[1] Average yearly rainfall is approximately 72 inches. During the rainy season from late May to October (called "winter" by Salvadoreans) the sun is frequently obscured by short and sometimes violent storms, rarely lasting more than a few hours. And in late August and September there are longer and heavier rains, known locally as *temporales*, that can blacken the skies for days and occasionally produce landslides and flooding at the lower elevations. The months from November to April are warmer and dryer, and Salvadoreans, though living in the Northern Hemisphere, refer to them as "summer."

The central plateau of El Salvador, running east to west and encompassing approximately 30 percent of the country's area, is dominated by a chain of relatively peaceful young volcanoes, which are

[1] See David Browning, *El Salvador: Landscape and society* (London, 1971), p. 3.

occasionally jolted to life by the earthquakes that continue to threaten the region. To the north and south of the central region lie older volcanic chains. Over time, these mountains have eroded, leaving a rugged terrain of high ridges, steep slopes, and narrow valleys that are now used for subsistence farming or grazing livestock.

The combination of a mild tropical climate and rich volcanic soil has made El Salvador a land of exceptional agricultural richness. Much of this land, in fact, was cultivated intensively in pre-Columbian times, and the Indian ancestors of today's small Salvadorean farmers had domesticated a wide range of plants by the time the white man arrived, including maize, beans, squash, pumpkin, avocado, tomato, cocoa, indigo, henequen, and tree cotton.[2] Not much is known about these early cultivators. In the western part of the country there survive pyramids believed to have been built by a people related to the Mayan culture that flourished in Guatemala and the Yucatán Peninsula of Mexico more than five centuries before Christ. As the Mayan civilization declined in El Salvador, it was replaced by Nahuatl-speaking peoples related to the powerful Aztec tribes of Mexico. This group, known by the local name "Pipil," at one time dominated approximately 70 percent of present-day El Salvador. Its territory ended at the Lempa River in the east, and beyond this the Lenca-speaking Indians, distant cousins of the Mayas, are believed to have retained control.

The Pipil subsisted chiefly on maize, using slash-and-burn methods to prepare the land for farming. Although their civilization never obtained the economic or political power of their Aztec cousins, it was sufficiently organized to support a number of urban centers, notably Cuscatlán, a city of more than 10,000 inhabitants that today forms part of San Salvador. Little is known about the day-to-day life of these cities or about the degree to which labor was specialized within the Pipil culture. However, the many weapons uncovered by archeologists suggest that wars must have been common among the various tribes. The prize of battle was undoubtedly El Salvador's rich agricultural land, and historians believe that competition for this was intense well before the Spanish conquest.[3]

[2] Browning, p. 5.
[3] Alastair White, *El Salvador* (New York, 1973), p. 23.

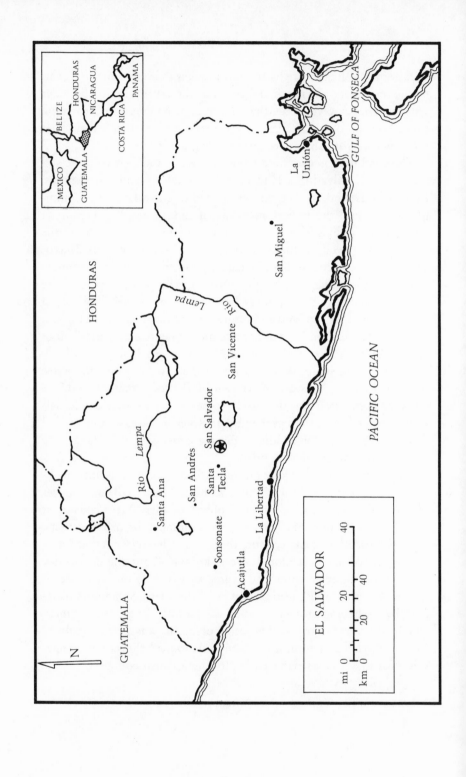

EL SALVADOR

GUATEMALA

HONDURAS

PACIFIC OCEAN

GULF OF FONSECA

Santa Ana

San Andrés

Sonsonate

Acajutla

Santa
Tecla

San Salvador

La Libertad

San Vicente

Río Lempa

Río Lempa

San Miguel

La
Unión

N

mi 0   20   40
km 0   20   40

MEXICO

BELIZE

GUATEMALA

HONDURAS

NICARAGUA

COSTA RICA

PANAMA

In 1524 Pedro de Alvarado, marching south from Mexico with some 200 Spanish soldiers and 3,000 Indian allies from Guatemala and Mexico, conquered the major Pipil tribes and claimed their territory for Spain. Subsequent expeditions were required to quell a few local rebellions, but by 1547 the Spanish grip was secure throughout the country. Unlike the British and French in North America, who treated Indians as an expendable enemy or occasional ally, the Spanish colonialists tried to integrate the native population into their European-oriented economy. For nearly 300 years what is now El Salvador was administered as part of the Captaincy-General of Guatemala. Cocoa, indigo, and Peru balsam were produced on plantations for export to Spain; and through systems of tribute (*encomienda*), forced labor (*repartimiento*), and debt slavery control over the best land was wrested from the small Indian farmers of the country. Yet these people's ties to the land were never completely destroyed. Even today, descendants of the Mayas still offer a special prayer before the planting season.

O god, my grandfather, my grandmother, god of the hills, god of the valleys, my holy god. I make you my offering with all my soul. Be patient with me in what I am doing. . . . It is needful that you give me . . . all I am going to sow here where I have my work, my cornfield. Watch it for me, guard it for me, let nothing happen to it from the time I sow it until I harvest it.[4]

The Indian and the Spaniard held fundamentally different and irreconcilable views of the land. The former, in geographer David Browning's words, "discovered, through experiment, the bountiful potential of his natural surroundings, and as a result of this knowledge perceived an intimate and meaningful relationship between man and the environment." The latter discovered, "through conquest, the possibilities for personal gain offered by a fertile land and its existing inhabitants, and viewed these two in terms of their exploitation."[5] Four hundred and fifty years after the Spanish conquest, and even though El Salvador's population has been homogenized by intermarriage and interbreeding among its racial groups, this essential conflict over the land and its use continues.

[4] J. Eric Thompson, *The rise and fall of Maya civilization* (London: 1956), as quoted in Browning, p. 7.
[5] Browning, p. 33.

DEMOGRAPHIC TRENDS

Present-day political and social conflicts in El Salvador are intensified by the fact that there is no longer enough arable land in the country to support its people, even if all titles were redistributed on a more equal basis. The nation's total population in 1974 was approximately 3.85 million, producing a population density of 470 per square mile—one of the highest in the Western Hemisphere and more than five times that of any other Central American country. El Salvador has none of the large undeveloped tracts of land that are still available for settlement elsewhere in Central America. Moreover, the population is expanding by 3.5 percent annually, outstripping the economy's ability to provide a decent standard of living for most of the people.

The cash-crop orientation of El Salvador's economy compounds the problem; but population growth in itself has created pressures that now threaten the very fabric of Salvadorean society. The effects of overpopulation are seen in virtually all aspects of national life. Basic food commodities have had to be imported in recent years, and even so studies of nutrition levels in the country reveal that the average Salvadorean does not receive either enough calories or enough protein.[6] It has been estimated that in rural areas nearly three-quarters of all children under five are affected by some form of dietary deficiency.

Employment is another problem area. Approximately 60 percent of El Salvador's active work force is engaged in agriculture. However, since most work is seasonal, the majority of these workers are underemployed, earning low wages and having little if any job security. A large part of the rural population is therefore forced to lead a nomadic existence in search of work. From November to March hands are needed to harvest coffee, cotton, and sugar; but if the rural Salvadorean male has no land upon which he can scratch out a living during the remaining months of the year, he must often abandon his family to seek whatever odd jobs he can find. Such factors account for the accelerated migration to El Salvador's cities in

[6] Inter-American Development Bank, *Social Progress Trust Fund: Ninth annual report* (Washington, 1969).

recent years, as well as for many social problems associated with an insecure life style—unstable marriages, a high rate of illegitimate births (63 percent of all Salvadoreans are born out of wedlock, according to latest estimates), and dangerous levels of violence and homicide.

Unemployment and the frustrations stemming from it are particularly acute in El Salvador's mountainous northern region, where the average family income is only $214 a year. This breaks down to an average monthly income of only $17.80 per family and $3.20 per capita, or about 10 cents a day.[7] In recent years, the hopelessness of life in this region has induced many Salvadoreans to slip across the frontier to Honduras, where land is both cheap and plentiful. This unrestrained and unsanctioned emigration was one of the factors that precipitated war between the two countries in July 1969. At the time hostilities broke out, 300,000 Salvadoreans were believed to be resident in Honduras—about 10 percent of the number of Salvadoreans living in their own country. These people, expelled by the Hondurans, were forced to seek refuge in El Salvador, compounding its population problems.

How El Salvador's economy will respond to the challenge of providing jobs, goods, and services to the bulk of the nation's citizens, who have so far been deprived of them, will determine, perhaps more than any other single factor, the health of the society and the future of its political institutions.

ECONOMIC PROFILE

The production of cash crops for export has been important in El Salvador for centuries. Even before the Spanish conquest, the Pipil and other local Indian cultures cultivated cocoa, which they traded for precious metals and other goods not found within their territory. Later, Spanish colonialists began exporting the native "Peru Balsam" (so named because it was transported in Peruvian ships), and introduced indigo, which remained a major source of foreign ex-

[7] These calculations, presented by the Subsecretary for Agriculture and Livestock, Francisco Lino Osequeda, at a Seminar on national agrarian reform conducted for officers of the Armed Forces (Aug. 26 through Sept. 1, 1973), appear on page 11.10.4 of the seminar report.

change until synthetic dyestuffs appeared at the end of World War I. Since about 1920, however, coffee has dominated both foreign trade and agricultural life within the country. It is not known exactly when the coffee plant was introduced into El Salvador, but small-scale production was noted in the early 1800's; and by 1875 coffee had surpassed indigo as an export crop. Despite El Salvador's recent efforts to diversify, coffee still accounts for more than half the value of the nation's total agricultural output.

Most of El Salvador's coffee is cultivated on large fincas (3,000-4,000 acres) spread out along the rich volcanic hillsides. Because young coffee plants do not become producing bushes for five years, constant attention is needed to ensure proper growth, and the grower's investment is an extended one. When the harvest begins, each tree must be picked over two or three times to guarantee that the berries collected have reached the proper ripeness. The raw berries are then taken to a processing center (*beneficio*), where a lengthy process of fermentation, drying, and milling occurs before the beans are examined by hand and placed in sacks for export.

The special needs of coffee production—lengthy cultivation, a large capital investment, and above all a seasonal supply of cheap labor for harvesting and processing—have had profound effects on El Salvador's economic and political life. Customs and laws governing land tenure were modified at the end of the last century so that the crop could be developed to its full potential on large estates. Railroads and highways were constructed to facilitate the transport of coffee out of the highlands, and ports were developed to ship it to foreign markets. The special taxes imposed on coffee exports soon became the largest single source of government revenue and politicians thus had a powerful incentive to champion the interests of large landowners over those of the thousands of itinerant laborers who worked on the plantations. As long as coffee remains El Salvador's main source of foreign exchange, it will tend to perpetuate a sharply stratified class structure and an uneven distribution of wealth within the country.

Cotton and sugar together have accounted for only a quarter of coffee's export earnings, but these crops do add some diversity to

El Salvador's agriculture.[8] The rise in cotton production along El Salvador's coastal plain since World War II is due mainly to two factors: the control of malaria in that region (which is unsuited for coffee production), and the balanced use of natural predators and chemical insecticides for the control of pests. Sugar production was begun by the first Spanish settlers, but only in recent years has the demand for refined white sugar, both in and outside El Salvador, become great enough to justify major capital improvements such as the construction of new mills and the purchase of more efficient machinery to harvest the crop. Both cotton and sugar, however, are still harvested predominantly by hand. And both are cultivated largely on the plateau and coastal lowlands, whereas coffee continues to dominate the mountain regions that contain El Salvador's richest cropland.

Overdependence on coffee, cotton, and sugar has increasingly troubled El Salvador's economic planners. All these crops require abundant cheap labor and large plantings to be farmed efficiently; moreover, a concentration on them places El Salvador in direct competition with other Third World nations that also have large unskilled labor forces and warm, tropical climates. To compete for a fair share of world trade in these crops, the country has been forced to maintain plantation agriculture, with its associated landowning elite and masses of poorly paid field hands.[9] Since the 1950's a growing intolerance for this state of affairs has been evident, and recent government policies have emphasized self-sufficiency and diversity in El Salvador's agriculture.

Food production has been given highest priority, so that the nutrition level of the population can be upgraded from its present position of next to last in the hemisphere.[10] (Also, government planners would like to cut down on food imports, which over the last decade

[8] Consejo Nacional de Planificación y Coordinación Económica (Conoplan), *Indicadores económica y sociales, September-December 1970, D.P. No. 819* (San Salvador, 1971), p. 121.

[9] David R. Raynolds, *Rapid development in small economies: The example of El Salvador* (New York, 1967), p. 19.

[10] *Economic Bulletin for Latin America* 17, No. 2 (New York: United Nations, 1973).

accounted for between 10 and 15 percent of the country's total imports.) To this end, and to reduce the dependence of El Salvador's foreign trade on a few cash crops, plans have been under way for some time to expand such things as the manufacture of farming supplies and the availability of rural credit institutions. Ultimately, however, to move the economy away from plantation farming the current pattern of landholdings must be reformed and the land itself redistributed. Although El Salvador has taken a few preliminary steps in this direction, much more must be done if the policy is to have any lasting effect.

Despite the continuing importance of agriculture in her economy, El Salvador is also the most highly industrialized country in Central America, and the percentage of her GNP stemming from manufacturing has been rising steadily in recent years. In 1969, the year war broke out with Honduras, the contribution of industry reached 19.6 percent, the highest in history, and that of agriculture reached its lowest point (25.9 percent).[11] The short war greatly reduced the volume of trade between Central American states, and the consequent recession was a severe blow to El Salvador's industrial sector, whose growth many viewed as largely dependent on an expansion of commercial ties within the region.

To some critics of El Salvador's industrialization policies, however, the expansion of markets, whether in Central America or elsewhere, would do little to solve the real development problems facing the country. It is claimed that consumer goods produced in El Salvador have already saturated the small existing market in Central America, and that the vast majority of people in the region are still too poor to buy them. If industrialization is to succeed, the argument continues, the internal market for Salvadorean products must increase through land reform and a more equal distribution of the country's wealth.[12] Only when the mass of people have secure jobs will they be able to participate in and enjoy the fruits of an industrial economy.

[11] See Manuel Zymelman, "Report on the feasibility of a manpower study for El Salvador" (presented to the Academy for Educational Development, Washington, D.C., 1971).

[12] White, pp. 228-29.

How jobs are to be provided is perhaps the most critical issue facing El Salvador at present. Although employment outside agriculture has accelerated during the last decade, the number of new jobs created has not kept pace with the rise in population. One reason is that industrialization carried out in El Salvador has tended to be capital-intensive. To turn out the most modern consumer goods—and probably to avoid labor troubles—Salvadorean entrepreneurs have customarily imported automated machinery developed in countries where labor is a major cost of production. Such technologies, say the critics, are grossly inappropriate in El Salvador, where there is a huge surplus of cheap labor.

Another problem facing Salvadorean industries is the supply of raw materials, and until quite recently almost all of these were imported from abroad. Under the 1968-72 Five-Year Plan, the development of El Salvador's own natural resources was encouraged, but it is not clear how far this policy can go. More likely, Salvadorean firms will take an intermediate role in world trade by importing raw or semifinished products and exporting finished goods. The recent opening of several electronics assembly factories is a step in this direction, and one that supports the often-heard wish of Salvadoreans that their country will someday be "the Japan of Central America."

POLITICAL TRENDS

El Salvador was the first province of New Spain to seize on the idea of ending Spanish domination. Father José Matias Delgado led an unsuccessful liberation movement in 1811, and another attempt was made in 1814 by Manuel José Arce. Mexico declared its independence in 1821, and Guatemala soon joined the Mexican Empire. El Salvador, however, opposed such a union, and went so far as to petition for admission to the United States. To bring her into line, Mexico and Guatemala sent their armies south and forced their recalcitrant neighbor to join the Empire. But after two years the five Central American nations north of Panama renounced Mexican rule and formed their own United Provinces of Central America, with Arce as their first president.

There was constant internal bickering between the five Provinces, and eventually it was decided to allow the members to form separate governments. Thus El Salvador became an independent republic in 1841. Bitter struggles continued within the country, and control of the government changed back and forth between liberals and conservatives until 1885, when the country thwarted the efforts of General Barrios of Guatemala to unify the region by force. A period of military rule under General Francisco Menéndez then began, lasting into the present century. El Salvador enjoyed comparative peace and considerable economic growth under civilian presidents from 1903 to 1931. When internal disputes surfaced in the late twenties, however, the military seized control again and army officers have occupied the presidency ever since.

On the surface such dramatic events would seem to connote major political change, if not chronic instability, but their net effect in El Salvador has been just the opposite. Throughout Salvadorean history, real economic and political power has been retained by a small aristocracy of wealthy landowners, either acting on their own or in coalition with the army. Only in the last 25 years have the pressures created by El Salvador's exploding population and the inadequacy of an economy based largely on coffee forced this elite to broaden its base and accept changes not wholly congruent with its own special interests.

More than any other factor, the exigencies of El Salvador's agricultural economy have determined the government's development policies. The land, most of which is still controlled by a small fraction of the population, came to be viewed as an estate entrusted to the coffee growers, and government policies were tailored to fit the needs of this group. By contrast, the wages and political rights of common agricultural workers were tightly controlled by the army. On the occasions when workers' grievances erupted into confrontation with the landholding elite, the government acted swiftly and often violently. Following a bloody uprising in western El Salvador in January 1932, for example, several thousand *campesinos* were massacred outright. This incident was followed by 14 years of dictatorial rule under General Maximiliano Hernández Martínez. Although government controls have relaxed somewhat in the three decades since his downfall, any challenges to authority or to the present pattern of land ownership are still dealt with swiftly and decisively, by force if necessary. Trade-union activity and leftist political activity have increased in El Salvador's urban areas since Hernández Martínez' time, but neither has ever been tolerated in the countryside.

In the years following World War II, El Salvador's military leaders have increasingly committed themselves to the kinds of development goals and programs embodied in numerous United Nations documents and in the Alliance for Progress. Industrialization, combined with a diversification and commercialization of agriculture, is now seen as the proper road to development. Private enterprise, it is hoped, will provide both the incentives and the mechanisms for growth in the "modern sectors"; meanwhile, the government will arrange favorable financial incentives, a stable currency, and such infrastructure services as roads, hospitals, and electrical power. This model also assigns the government a limited role in providing social services such as housing and health care to people who are unable to provide for themselves; however, these programs are intended to supplement private sector activities, not to interfere or compete with them. Universal primary education is supported by the government, although families who can afford it may send their children to private schools.

For some time El Salvador relied on international market forces to guide her economy, and this strategy was favored by the country's coffee interests. In the 1950's, however, when the growth of the economy was threatened by overdependence on a few agricultural exports, the state intervened to establish definite development priorities. Industrialization was championed because it would provide diversity and would ensure the nation a pivotal position within the Central American community and in any future common market arrangement that might evolve there. In some ways this was not a new aspiration: in the years following independence from Spain, El Salvador had been the strongest advocate of Central American union; and she has been the foremost advocate of regional trade agreements, in the hope that such policies would provide new markets for Salvadorean products and jobs for thousands of idle workers.

Absorption of surplus population is perhaps the key concept underlying current development policy. Already, thousands of Salvadoreans have migrated to the cities, where their lack of education or skills has perpetuated their unemployment and contributed to growing social tension. Only through the creation of new job opportunities and the mobilization of these unused human resources, government leaders believe, can they head off increased social unrest and build a viable economy in the years ahead. Although these policies have not yet been formally elaborated in any detail, they are implicit in the country's Educational Reform and in the use of instructional television—the subject of this book. Should present demographic trends continue, however, neither the growth nor the absorption rate of the modern sectors will keep pace with the increase in population. All this suggests that more radical political changes may be in store for El Salvador in the years ahead.

EDUCATION BEFORE THE 1967 REFORM

Little attention was paid to formal education in El Salvador under the Spanish. Traditionally, knowledge was passed from one generation to the next during day-to-day activities at home and in the fields, and what little formal instruction existed was controlled by religious bodies. (Even in pre-Columbian times Indian priests in the region had maintained schools associated with their temples.) The efforts of Catholic priests and missionaries were extremely limited. When the bishop of Guatemala visited San Salvador in 1770, he was astonished to find "not a single grammar [secondary] school, nor even one for the teaching of reading, writing, and the Christian doctrine."[13]

Following independence, interest in education grew, and the nation's first secondary school and university were founded. Besides encouraging municipal authorities to establish primary schools, the government also set salary levels for teachers and drew up standard curricula, initially including courses in reading, writing, arithmetic, morals, and civics. Educational policy remained unchanged until 1887, when a group of visiting Colombian educators recommended the expanded use of textbooks to replace oral recitation, the adop-

[13] Francisco Espinosa, as quoted in Cameron D. Ebaugh, *Education in El Salvador* (Washington: GPO, 1947), p. 6.

tion of a sixth-grade primary school, and the assignment of a single teacher to each grade.[14] In subsequent reforms around the turn of the century, kindergartens were founded in the larger towns and manual arts training was added to the primary curriculum. In the late 1920's, the first vacation courses for teachers were organized, and coeducation was begun with the founding of several "consolidated" rural schools. Coeducation in particular was a radical educational innovation for its time, and it has still not been adopted in all other Latin American countries.

The school calendar in El Salvador is organized around the harvest schedule. The coffee and cotton crops are brought in from November through January, and entire families often migrate to the plantation to work as pickers. Hence the academic year usually starts around the third week of January and lasts to the end of October; but a late harvest can set this schedule back.

In 1940 a debate began about whether education should be made more available and more relevant to the country's masses. Alternatives to the time-honored classical curriculum, rote memorization, and other existing methods of instruction were proposed. But the established patterns did not die easily. They were defended by conservatives both inside and outside the Ministry of Education, who were products of the old system and who resisted policies designed to take individual student needs, abilities, and personalities into account. At the heart of the resistance was the traditional view that knowledge and information are inherently scarce resources, which must be dispensed sparingly and only to people who are qualified and who are willing to make the necessary sacrifices to obtain them. Historically, the rewards for these sacrifices were the primary, secondary, and university diplomas, each connoting different job possibilities and a different niche in the country's social hierarchy. The fact that these conservative educational patterns lasted so long in El Salvador suggests that the relationship between the school system and the interests of the society's coffee-growing elite was a strong one.

[14] Espinosa, as quoted in Ebaugh, pp. 6-7.

CHAPTER TWO

ITV and the Educational Reform

Educational reform became an important issue in El Salvador during the 1960's. A number of prominent citizens in the government and elsewhere concluded that a comprehensive upgrading of the school system and the creation of new educational opportunities were essential if the country was to resolve its pressing economic and social problems. Such thinking also underlay the political rhetoric of the 1967 presidential campaign, during which Colonel Fidel Sanchez Hernández, the candidate of the dominant Partido de Conciliación Nacional (PCN), promised to reform the educational system if elected. Following his election, Sanchez Hernández appointed as his Minister of Education Walter Béneke, a former ambassador and businessman. Under Béneke's leadership, a reform commission was established to evaluate El Salvador's educational system and to propose changes.

Although Salvadorean law requires all children to attend primary school, in the years immediately preceding the Educational Reform fewer than one child in seven who began school ever graduated from the sixth grade. The legal starting age of seven years for first grade was only loosely adhered to: a few children entered early; many entered late. El Salvador's educational pyramid is a steep one, as the enrollment for 1967 illustrates (see Table 2.1). Nearly half a million students were enrolled in grades one through nine, but over half of them were in the first and second grades. The high dropout and repeater rates that produced this imbalance stemmed from shortcomings in the rural areas, as well as from the highly punitive grading

TABLE 2.1
Enrollment in Grades 1-9 in 1967

Grade	Enrollment (thousands)[a]	Percent of total enrollment	Grade	Enrollment (thousands)	Percent of total enrollment
1	158.5	32.63%	6	31.3	6.44%
2	99.8	20.54	7[b]	13.8	2.84
3	69.9	14.39	8[b]	10.4	2.14
4	54.0	11.12	9[b]	8.5	1.75
5	39.6	8.15			

SOURCE: *Estudios de la matrícula diurna en educatión primaria y secundaria 1968–1975.* San Salvador: CONOPLAN, April 1968.

[a] Includes both public and private schools.

[b] Grades 7–9 were traditionally known as the Plan Básico; under the reform they became the Third Cycle of Basic Education. In 1967 tuition and incidental fees were still required of students in these grades, and enrollment in them was not compulsory.

and promotion policies applied throughout the system. According to the Reform Commission's survey, two-thirds of all rural schools did not offer all six primary grades, and 60 percent of them had only one room and one teacher.

A second factor contributing to the high attrition rate among students was the inappropriateness of the curricula which were based on values and concepts imported from Europe in the nineteenth century. The curricula provided little practical guidance for teachers, and courses were overloaded with inconsequential facts at every grade level, prompting Minister Béneke to remark that they were designed to produce "human archives"—students who were forced to memorize information with little practical relationship to the needs of the country or the individual. Since the curricula were predominantly humanistic, and thus useful chiefly to the elite minority of students destined for the university, students who terminated their schooling at lower levels were ill-prepared to assume any productive role in their society. The narrow focus of the secondary school curricula in particular was a bottleneck in El Salvador's development, and was hardly designed to meet the need for middle-level technicians and managers who could work effectively in industry and commercial agriculture.

The Ministry of Education itself was burdened with an administrative apparatus that could not deal adequately with existing problems, much less anticipate new ones. Its 22 departments were scattered among 20 different buildings in San Salvador. The resulting inefficiency may be illustrated by the imbalance that had developed in training and placing new teachers. The primary normal schools were producing graduates far in excess of the system's ability to absorb them (in 1967 approximately 2,000 primary teachers were unemployed), yet the normal schools themselves were continuing to expand. At the same time, according to Ministry estimates, four out of five teachers working at the secondary level, or Plan Básico (grades 7-9), had not completed the advanced studies supposedly required to instruct at that level. Such imbalances resulted because there was insufficient communication and planning between Ministry departments. And the school system in general was not expanding fast enough either to employ new teachers or to provide a basic primary education for all of El Salvador's youth.

The payment and supervision of classroom teachers was another serious administrative problem, particularly at the secondary level. Secondary teachers were paid on an hourly basis; and many in the urban areas gained extra income by teaching at a number of different schools simultaneously, dashing from one to another between classes. These "taxi teachers" seldom had time to work with their students outside of class. District supervisors could do little to prevent such abuses, and in fact played mostly a record-keeping role in El Salvador's school system before the Reform. Responsible for 40 or more schools, the typical supervisor was burdened with a wide range of legal and jurisdictional disputes he was not properly trained to handle, which usually prevented him from doing much to improve the quality of classroom instruction. Politics also biased the supervisors' actions. The Reform's planners were anxious to convert the school supervisor from a harried inspector to a more objective technical adviser and pedagogical consultant.

ELEMENTS OF THE EDUCATIONAL REFORM

To remedy the numerous problems that had been inherited from previous administrations and to streamline an educational system whose goals and procedures had ceased to fit the needs of El Salvador, Minister Béneke set forth a comprehensive five-year reform plan in the spring of 1968. His approach was systematic and thorough, touching virtually every aspect of the educational system. The major programs included:

1. Reorganization of the Ministry of Education.
2. Teacher retraining.
3. Curriculum revision.
4. Development of new teachers' guides and student workbooks.
5. Improvement of school supervision to provide "advice" instead of inspection.
6. Development of a wider diversity of technical training programs in grades 10-12.
7. Extensive remodeling and construction of schools.
8. Elimination of tuition in grades 7-9.
9. Use of double sessions to teach more pupils. (The single-session schedule of 7-11 A.M. and 1:30-4 P.M. was replaced in most schools by a morning shift of 7-12 and an afternoon shift of 1-6.)
10. A new student evaluation system, incorporating changes in promotion and grading policies.
11. A "teachers' law" that standardized the number of classroom hours required of each teacher and set a new pay scale.
12. Installation of a national instructional television system for grades 7-9.

Although some of the reforms were undertaken immediately, most were begun with the understanding that additional planning, experimentation, and adjustment would be required, and that the major changes would have to come gradually. However, the five-year timetable was a strict one; in fact, it coincided with the single term of President Sanchez Hernández, and Minister Béneke was intent on carrying it through without bureaucratic opposition or delay.

This study of instructional television (ITV) in El Salvador was complicated by the fact that it was but one element of the ambitious Educational Reform. For this reason, the character of the other reform programs, their schedule of implementation, and their particular relationship to television were all basic concerns of the evaluation.[1]

---

[1] Four sources were used to examine television's special role in the Reform. The first included documents published by the Ministry of Education and specifying the nature of the various Reform programs. Records of the U.S. Agency for

EARLY HISTORY OF THE ITV SYSTEM

Although the introduction of expensive and technologically complex educational innovations would seem to require considerable
forethought and planning, the histories of instructional television
projects throughout the world have in fact been characterized by
undue haste. Educational authorities, impatient to get their television systems working, have tended to rush through the planning
stage in order to get studios constructed and programs on the air.
Moreover, the needs of teachers and the conditions in their classrooms have generally been neglected or given insufficient attention,
and as a result weaknesses have been built into ITV systems from
the outset. All the oversights, however, eventually return to haunt
the administrators of new television systems and to undermine the
effectiveness of their programs.

In contrast to many projects elsewhere, the decision to use television in El Salvador was neither imposed from the outside nor taken
in a precipitous fashion. Beginning about 1960, the possibility of
starting some form of educational broadcasting was raised in the
country's press. The small size of El Salvador and the fact that virtually all the people are Spanish-speaking were favorable factors
cited by a number of prominent citizens who were interested in the
potential of television as an educational tool. Although these early
advocates were aware of El Salvador's educational problems—the
high rate of illiteracy, insufficient school facilities, high repeater and
dropout rates—there was little real knowledge among them of how

International Development (USAID) were a second source of archival material;
these included the original ITV feasibility studies, loan agreements signed by El
Salvador and the United States, and monthly reports and administrative memo-
randa submitted by the U.S. professionals hired to help in various Reform programs. The firsthand knowledge and experience that the Stanford evaluation team
itself gained from close association with the Reform over four years was a third
source of administrative data. The team participated in many meetings with
Ministry officials and attended the weekly staff briefings held by USAID's education officers. Finally, to explore in depth the information obtained from reviewing formal documents and to validate the insights gained through partici-
pant observation, interviews of Ministry personnel and their foreign advisers
were conducted. The advisers were customarily interviewed at the end of their
tours of duty; the Salvadoreans were interviewed during the summer of 1971
and again at the end of the 1972 school year.

television might help eradicate such problems. Above all, the country at that time lacked the capital and expertise necessary to initiate any large television project.

The initiative that led directly to the establishment of El Salvador's national ITV system was taken by Walter Béneke in 1961. Then ambassador to Japan, Béneke was impressed by the role television played in that country's correspondence high schools. Anxious to stimulate the growth of something similar in his own country, he sought the help of NHK, the Japan Broadcasting Corporation. NHK agreed to conduct a feasibility study, and several engineers were dispatched to El Salvador for that purpose in 1962. The results of the study confirmed what Béneke had suspected: El Salvador possessed almost ideal topographical conditions for the installation of a national television system (see Figure 2.1).

The initiative taken by Béneke was supported by President Julio Adalberto Rivera, who established the first Educational Television Commission in 1963. The Commission was asked to evaluate alternative uses for educational television, with the goal of proposing a national plan. However, the group met sporadically, and little progress was made until 1965, when Béneke returned from his ambassadorship. Under his chairmanship weekly meetings were instituted, and the Commission made a fresh start. Throughout 1966, it debated the ways in which television might best serve El Salvador's educational needs, though how those needs were defined depended largely on the experience and particular interests of the Commission's individual members. A strong case was made for using home television to extend the school, delivering basic education and literacy programs to adults and young dropouts who had never completed the sixth grade. Other members of the Commission favored using television exclusively within the formal school system, although there was disagreement on whether it would be more useful at the primary or the secondary level.

By the end of 1966 a consensus had been reached on several basic points. First, acknowledging that El Salvador did not have the trained people or economic resources needed to undertake a large television project, the Commission decided that its initial efforts would have to be limited in scale but flexible enough to permit expansion should

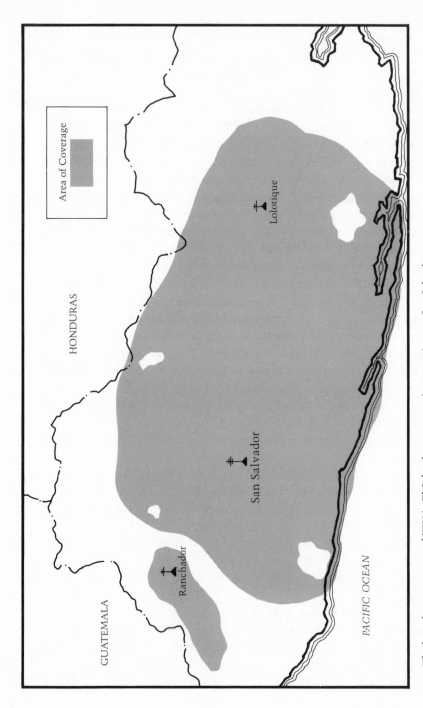

2.1. The broadcast coverage of ITV in El Salvador, 1972; main transmitter at San Salvador, with repeaters at Ranchador and Lolotique (data from Dirección de Television Educativa, Nueva San Salvador)

circumstances permit. Second, the Plan Básico (grades 7-9) was selected as the first level to be served by television, for the lack of opportunity and low quality of instruction at this level were believed to be retarding El Salvador's industrial development. The Commission members believed that instructional television would help compensate for the many unqualified secondary school teachers, who could be trained in a short time as effective monitors within television classes. Third, the Commission concluded that ITV should be administered by a new executive agency with freedom to set its own policies unencumbered by existing ministerial procedures. Finally, it was resolved to seek foreign financial and technical assistance so that ITV could be put on as firm a footing as possible from the outset.

The World Bank displayed some interest in El Salvador's preliminary plans during this period, and a feasibility study conducted on its behalf in 1967 reached the same favorable conclusions as the earlier Japanese study. Members of the ETV Commission were optimistic that a World Bank loan could be obtained to launch the project. Their plans changed, however, when president-elect Sanchez Hernández attended a conference of Western Hemisphere presidents at Punta del Este, Uruguay, in March 1967. There he heard President Lyndon Johnson set forth a U.S. proposal to sponsor pilot ITV programs in Latin America.[2] Sanchez Hernández realized that El Salvador could qualify for such assistance; and upon his return he urged the Commission to put its case before officials of the U.S. Agency for International Development (USAID).

USAID, which had already come to consider El Salvador a prime candidate for the implementation for President Johnson's proposal, displayed an immediate interest in the Salvadorean request. In the late spring of 1967, a team of experts under contract to the National Association of Educational Broadcasters arrived in El Salvador to conduct yet another feasibility study. The six-man team confirmed the technical feasibility of a national television system in El Salvador and found many other circumstances favoring the establishment of such a system, including strong support within the Ministry of Ed-

[2] President Johnson's proposal stemmed from a recommendation of his White House Task Force on ETV in the Less Developed Countries, which had been established in November 1966 under the chairmanship of Leonard Marks.

ucation and indications that the Salvadorean government intended
to undertake some educational broadcasting with its own resources.[3]
It was recommended that USAID respond favorably to the Salvadorean request.

Substantial differences emerged during USAID's subsequent discussions with Salvadorean leaders concerning what kind of project
should be undertaken. Reflecting the priorities of President Johnson's
ETV Task Force, the USAID representatives encouraged the Salvadoreans to give televised instruction as full a test as possible—one
that could become a genuine showcase for the rest of the hemisphere.
In accord with this view, USAID believed that television would have
the greatest impact at the primary level, where six out of seven Salvadorean students were still enrolled. The Salvadoreans felt that a
project at the primary level would be difficult, given the costs of
such a system and their country's lack of experience. They also put
forward a strong case for beginning televised instruction with the
Plan Básico, where they saw the greatest need. Eventually, it was
agreed to begin a project in the Plan Básico, extending it to other
grades if it proved successful.

Also at issue during the early stages of ITV was where to place
overall responsibility for the new system. The Salvadoreans, aware
of the many bureaucratic obstacles within their own Ministry of Education, argued for a new executive agency directly under the president. Only in this manner, they felt, would it be possible to avoid
red tape during the procurement of equipment and the hiring of personnel. The USAID representatives, on the other hand, were wary
of granting the project too much administrative autonomy. They believed that although freedom in the areas of purchasing and recruit-
ment would indeed be desirable, close collaboration with the Ministry of Education was absolutely essential in the long run if TV was
to be integrated into the school system. For this reason, USAID
argued that ITV should be developed within the Ministry, where
planning could be carried out in conjunction with the officials who
had jurisdiction over Salvadorean schools. The debate was not settled on the merits of this argument, however, but rather by the for-

[3] NAEB, *The feasibility of using television for educational development in
El Salvador* (Washington: 1967)

tuitous naming of Béneke as Minister of Education in July 1967, which ensured that ITV would receive strong support at the highest level.

Despite the fact that ITV enjoyed a high priority within El Salvador's Educational Reform, school broadcasts did not actually begin until February 1969, 19 months after Béneke had taken office. The delay was necessary to provide adequate production facilities, to recruit and train personnel, and to delineate ITV's role and responsibilities in relation to those of the older, established divisions of the Ministry of Education.

PRODUCTION FACILITIES

Of primary importance to the Salvadorean government was the construction of a production center to serve the ITV system. For over a year the ITV division of the Ministry of Education produced experimental programs and conducted its training courses in the studios of one of San Salvador's two commercial television stations. The perpetuation of this arrangement was deemed unsatisfactory for many reasons. Because the station broadcast mostly imported programs, its own production facilities were quite modest and did not meet the needs of the ITV producers and directors. The shortage of film equipment and graphic arts production, in particular, severely limited the approaches ITV directors could take in their subject areas.

From their earliest association with the project, the USAID representatives were also convinced of the need to provide the emerging ITV system with a home of its own. Under the terms of the project agreement signed by USAID and the government of El Salvador, the Salvadoreans agreed to construct and maintain a production center. In turn, USAID agreed to donate equipment. In addition to studio equipment (lights, cameras, videotape recorders, etc.), USAID provided film equipment, graphic arts materials, and the printing machinery necessary to produce teachers' guides and student workbooks. USAID also supplied transmission equipment and 100 television receivers; all told, its contribution to the start-up costs of the ITV system amounted to $653,000.

The USAID grant was made on the condition that during the first

year of school broadcasting (1969) the Salvadoreans would themselves undertake the expansion of their production capability. This
was to be financed by a loan of $1.9 million from USAID, which
would provide for the equipping of a second production studio and
the purchase of additional television receivers. Also included in the
second phase would be the purchase of enough transmission equipment to give the ITV system two channels of its own. With this
added capability, an estimated 90 percent of the country's secondary
schools could be reached by the broadcast signal.

The loan funds should have become available early in 1969, per-
mitting the construction of a second studio in time for the 1970
school year. But the Salvadorean National Assembly, which had to
approve and then authorize the spending of the loan, did not act on
the matter until late May of 1969; this meant that the new studio
could not possibly be ready before January of the following year.
Moreover, when El Salvador and Honduras went to war in July 1969
aid funds to both countries were frozen by the United States. The
freeze was not lifted until the beginning of 1970, by which time the
ITV system was a year behind its expansion timetable. Still more
delay was caused by the Salvadorean Assembly. Although it had
previously approved a general loan agreement, debate over the details
of that agreement postponed final authorization for another year.
When authorization was finally granted in October 1970, ITV was
effectively two years behind schedule.

Despite these numerous delays, the ITV staff adapted quite well
to the situation. By adopting program production schedules that kept
the single existing studio operating 12 hours a day, and by leasing
the transmission facilities of both of San Salvador's commercial TV
stations, the production teams were able to meet their videotaping
schedules, and service was extended on time to all three Third Cycle
grades.

In October 1971, a full year after the Assembly had authorized the
disbursement of the ITV loan, the addition of a second studio was
still far in the future, although a new building had been completed
to house both the original studio and the new one. The machinery
of the Salvadorean government was unable to cope effectively with
the USAID procedures for drawing up specifications for new equip-

ment. As a result, soliciting bids from foreign manufacturers and actually ordering new equipment took many months, and the cumbersome bureaucracy of the government procurement office (the Corte de Cuentas) ensnarled ITV's leaders in endless red tape.

Another problem stemmed from the fact that the Salvadoreans themselves had neither participated in nor learned from the experience of equipping the first ITV studio, which had been arranged largely by USAID personnel. When problems arose concerning the ordering of additional equipment or spare parts, the U.S. advisers were relied upon; indeed, they purchased virtually all major equipment and parts during the project's first two years. This practice prevented the Salvadoreans from gaining vital technical experience in many areas of their own project.

The location of the original ITV studio was another issue that created administrative difficulties during the early years of the ITV system. During the feasibility studies, various sites had been considered, the main criterion being that the studio had to be constructed on government land. The choices were eventually narrowed to two: Santa Tecla, a large town on the outskirts of the capital; and San Andrés, the site of a rural normal school that had been constructed with USAID funds in the mid-1960's but had never been utilized and was something of an embarrassment to the Ministry of Education. Two factors favored the placement of the ITV center at San Andrés. First, part of the normal school could be remodeled for television production, removing a white elephant from the consciences of both Ministry and USAID planners. Second, under the Educational Reform, San Andrés was also to be the site of the new national teacher training program. Ministry planners believed that placing the new ITV studio at San Andrés would foster close interaction between the TV production teams and the teachers who would ultimately be using the televised lessons in the classroom. It was hoped that a cross-fertilization of ideas would result.

Despite its advantages, San Andrés had certain liabilities as a production center. Its distance from San Salvador (15 miles) created a problem, since all of the ITV staff lived in the capital. Bus service was provided, but nearly an hour was consumed getting to or from San Andrés. The distance also made it difficult to obtain spare parts

The Santa Tecla production center, studio building in the background

or other materials from San Salvador at short notice. San Andrés personnel had difficulty holding other teaching jobs or pursuing their own studies after work hours—two patterns that were very common among the teachers who made up over 85 percent of the ITV staff. And communication between the ITV division and Ministry offices in the capital was difficult because the single telephone line from San Andrés to San Salvador was in frequent need of repair.

San Andrés was located at a lower altitude than San Salvador, and the difference was enough to account for considerable physical discomfort. In addition to the heat, high humidity during the wet season and dust during the dry season caused serious maintenance problems for the studio engineers, particularly during the first broadcast year. The air conditioning system presented numerous problems because it had to be run at full force most of the time. To further complicate matters, electric power and water services were highly erratic. The frequent loss of power interrupted the taping of programs on an average of three times a week during the first three years, and the periodic curtailment of water service endangered health and lowered staff morale.

It was neither the isolation nor the physical discomfort of the San Andrés campus, however, that ultimately prompted the project's leaders to move production facilities to a new location; rather, there was simply no compelling reason to stay there. Despite the intentions of the project's planners (and for reasons that will be discussed below), a productive working relationship never developed between the San Andrés normal school and the adjoining ITV center. Had cooperation existed during the first few years of the reform, there would have been stronger pressure to maintain the association, even though most of the Plan Básico teachers who were retrained under the Reform had completed their programs by the end of 1971.

In the original plan, as we have seen, the second studio was to have been installed at San Andrés during 1969. This timetable was scrapped owing to the long delay of the USAID loan. Midway through the 1970 school year, when the planners discovered that the costs of constructing a new facility would not be prohibitive compared to those of simply expanding the existing center, the decision was taken to move the whole operation to Santa Tecla. The television production facility moved to its new home in February 1972, and installation of the second studio was completed at the end of that year—three school years behind the original timetable.

RECRUITMENT AND TRAINING OF THE ITV STAFF

One feature that distinguished the Salvadorean ITV system from those in other countries was that major responsibility rested in native hands from the very beginning. In the ITV systems founded in Ivory Coast, Niger, and American Samoa, for example, foreign advisers were in charge of setting up the studios and producing the first series of programs. As the systems grew, more local people were taken on, but the advisers retained a disproportionate control over the direction of the projects. In El Salvador, highly motivated foreign advisers played instrumental roles in getting various aspects of the ITV system off the ground, but final Salvadorean authority over the system was never in question. This fact built confidence within the Salvadorean staff and contributed to the rapid expansion of televised instruction in the schools.

As mentioned previously, the prospect of a large ITV system did not become imminent until the formal project agreement was signed by El Salvador and the United States in spring 1968. At that time, the ITV section of the Ministry of Education contained less than 20 people, mostly classroom teachers who had no formal training in television teaching techniques. The experimental programming they had initiated in 1967 with some help from UNESCO had given them a rudimentary knowledge of television production, but it had not prepared them for the rigors of a full production schedule. Moreover, they had no cameramen, filmmakers, or graphic artists—talents that had hitherto been "borrowed" from one of San Salvador's commercial stations. It was clear to the project's leaders that these specialized skills would have to be provided before serious programming could begin; the problem was that few Salvadoreans possessed them, and even fewer were willing to leave their better-paying jobs with the commercial broadcasters.

At first, only employees of the Ministry of Education were considered for positions in its new ITV division. This meant that the vast majority of the teleteachers, directors, and technicians were drawn from the existing teacher corps. Thus the new division could be assembled without straining the Ministry's budget; and, as former teachers, the new ITV staff would presumably have a firsthand knowledge of the conditions and needs of their nation's schools. A large number of classroom teachers had expressed an early interest in ITV, and there was no trouble in attracting many candidates for the new jobs.

It was difficult to identify the best possible people for the new ITV positions, however, since none of the candidates already had the training or experience required to function effectively as a television teacher, director, or writer of teaching guides. To narrow the field, a heavy emphasis was placed on academic background, and all members of the production teams were required to be graduates of the Superior Normal School. In addition, achievement tests were administered to select those with the greatest knowledge of the subjects to be taught on television. To choose potential teleteachers, there was also a screen test to evaluate general appearance, voice quality, and stage presence. Candidates who excelled on the tests were assigned positions on the eventual production teams. Regret-

A program team at work in the control room; the director of the lesson is at center

The studio crew prepares to broadcast

Minister Béneke (pointing) shows officials a student project honoring the Educational Reform; President Sanchez Hernández is at the Minister's right

A teacher at the retraining center practices his delivery with the help of a portable videotape unit and a studio monitor

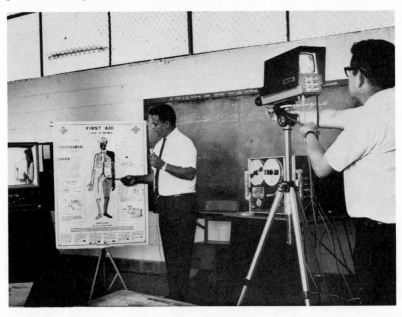

tably, almost all the specialties assigned were permanent, and little effort was made to review or modify assignments during the first two years of broadcasting. In retrospect, this policy seems unnecessarily rigid, especially since 1969 was to have been a "pilot" year, during which changes were to be made to achieve the best possible working combinations of the various production jobs (lesson planner, teleteacher, etc.).

Finding qualified people for the studio crews of the ITV system proved to be even more challenging, since these jobs did not require formal academic training so much as practical experience and know-how. Unfortunately, an adequate method for evaluating and recruiting technical personnel was not arrived at in the project's early years. Instead, primary school teachers were used to fill such positions as cameraman and switcher, and they were given only minimum training before being put to work. The majority of teachers, directors, and writers in the production teams were also forced to learn on the job. This sink-or-swim situation did have one clear advantage: it generated pride and taught the production teams that they could get the job done. Their self-confidence might have been retarded had the Salvadoreans relied on the usual practice of letting foreign advisers take charge until local personnel could be prepared thoroughly through an apprenticeship program.

On-the-job training also had certain negative effects. Above all, it made the organization of a continuous supplemental training program for the staff very difficult (this was one of the great frustrations voiced by the foreign advisers during the first three years). Pressured by a rigorous production schedule, most members of the ITV staff regarded time devoted exclusively to training as a waste. Similarly, the criterion for success became not the quality of the lessons produced, but rather the number of lessons produced on schedule.

Although members of the production teams received very little formal training after they began taping programs, the courses they were required to attend before qualifying for a position on the ITV staff gave them a rudimentary knowledge of television production techniques. Unfortunately, the same cannot be said for the teachers who worked on the studio crew, operating the cameras, lights, and sound equipment with only the simplest of instructions. Over time, this group was expected to master the operation of complicated equipment and to respond professionally to technical direction from the control room. And by the end of the first year they were working in a reasonably efficient manner, although many programs had to be remade because of technical errors that might have been avoided had more attention been given to orientation and training. During the third year of broadcasting (1971) the administrators of the ITV Division began to realize that additional training was needed if program quality was to improve.

Having successfully met the challenge of producing an average of three lessons a week, each production team now began exploring ways to use television in more imaginative and effective ways. They became more interested in the student learning associated with different teaching strategies and, accordingly, in the feedback from classrooms that were using their programs. Before the 1972 school year, the entire ITV staff participated in daily training seminars and laboratory exercises derived from existing theories of teaching with television, and experimentation with new instructional design techniques was encouraged throughout the following year. As a result of these projects, the ITV Division created the post of Director of Educational Broadcast Quality, which had as its primary function the upgrading of quality through better lesson planning, the use of behavioral objectives, and the pretesting of programs.

COORDINATION OF TASKS WITHIN THE ITV DIVISION

Production for educational television requires, above all, the effective coordination of diverse tasks and talents. Scripts must be ready far enough in advance so that graphic artists and film crews can prepare the appropriate visual materials; rehearsal time must be sufficient for the television teachers to become thoroughly familiar with their scripts; and the accompanying classroom materials for each lesson must be prepared and distributed well in advance of its transmission date. Obviously, the coordination of these activities must be precise if high-quality lessons are to be produced. Many of the administrative problems encountered in this area during ITV's early years were caused by the complexity of the system itself and by the inexperience of the project's staff. These problems can best be understood in terms of the work carried out by the individual production teams.

In the first year of broadcasting (1969), each production team was responsible for one seventh-grade series—math, social studies, natural science, Spanish, or English. A team included five persons: two subject specialists, a television teacher, a producer-director, and a production assistant or "coordinator." With few exceptions, all these positions were filled by former classroom teachers.

The subject specialists were responsible for the basic content of the broadcasts, and worked from the official curriculum to prepare an outline of the learning objectives to be achieved in a particular television course, as well as the specific concepts to be covered in each lesson. They were also responsible for preparing the accompanying classroom teaching guides and student workbooks. The teacher prepared his own script from the subject guidelines and presented it on the air. The producer-director was in charge of everything that happened in the studio—teacher's performance, studio sets, camera angles, duration of scenes, and so on. The production coordinator was responsible for assembling the visual materials needed for each program (charts, models, slides, or film clips), and for inviting the guests who occasionally appeared on some series.

This description may give the impression of a highly fragmented production scheme; but the teams themselves discovered in the first year of broadcasting that the secret to successful programming lay in common planning and preparation for each lesson. Through experience, the teachers and subject specialists in particular found they had to work closely together if the lessons, guides, and workbooks were to complement one another.

Originally, each production team was responsible for three or four programs a week, but this number was gradually reduced to two or three (see Table 2.2). The cutback reflected in part the need to crowd production for three grades into a single studio, in part a need to use air time as economically as possible, and in part a rethinking of the optimum number of lessons that could be utilized effectively in the schools.

More serious problems arose in coordinating the work of the pro-

TABLE 2.2
TV Classes per Week per Subject

Subject	1969 (grade 7 only)	1970 (grades 7 & 8)	1971 (grades 7, 8, & 9)[a]	1972 (grades 7, 8, & 9)
Spanish	4 (3)[b]	2	2	2
Social studies	4 (3)	3	2 (3)[c]	2 (3)
Science	4 (3)	3	3	3
Mathematics	4 (3)	3	3	3
English	3	3	3	3

[a] In the ninth grade in 1971 there were no ITV programs after July.
[b] After June 1969 programming in all subjects was reduced to three classes per subject.
[c] Grades 8 and 9 received only two social studies classes per week via ITV in 1971 and 1972, whereas the seventh grade received three.

duction teams with that of other sections of the ITV Division, given the lack of understanding between sections, the lack of effective leadership from above, and the constant pressure of time. For example, one major problem was the excess demand of the production teams on the film and graphics sections. It was clear throughout the first two years of broadcasting that the production teams had no realistic concept of the time required to prepare artwork. Their last-minute orders for individual programs proved impossible to fill in many instances, and this resulted in bitterness and accusations that the graphics section was not doing its job. Similar charges were leveled at the film section, which was short of skilled personnel and had no film-processing equipment of its own until the second year of taping. These handicaps prevented the film crews from filling many orders on time. But the production teams tended to ignore this, continued to make unrealistic requests, and frequently lost their tempers when the requests were not met.

To the credit of the ITV system, coordination among the various sections improved as the project grew. A new subdirector was put in charge of day-to-day operations, leaving the director free to concentrate on institutional organization and longer-range policies.

ITV AND OTHER EDUCATIONAL REFORMS

The ITV system, thrust into the forefront of El Salvador's Educational Reform, had considerable influence on the content of the other programs, and particularly on their rate of development. By the time other elements of the Reform began to take shape in 1968, the Division of Educational Television had been operating for two years and had already produced some experimental programs. Because the Ministry of Education insisted that televised instruction must not be started ahead of the concomitant reforms in other areas, there was great pressure on other divisions of the Ministry to keep pace with television's timetable. On the whole, they were successful.

Enrollment

The planners of El Salvador's Educational Reform concentrated their efforts initially on grades 7-9 because they viewed the existing deficiencies at this level as major impediments to their goal of speeding economic development through the improved training and utilization of the nation's human resources. In 1971, the third year of the Reform, the Ministry of Education declared that all Salvadoreans were entitled to nine grades of schooling, and that a crash program was needed to increase the absorptive capacity of grades 7-9, which were designated the Third Cycle of Basic Education.

In quantitative terms, the seventh-grade enrollment "bottleneck" was removed in a very short time. When the Reform began in 1968, approximately 20,000 students were enrolled in grades 7-9 of the public schools and some 23,000 in the private schools. These students were less than 25 percent of the number of young people of eligible age (13-15) for the three grades. Starting in 1971, the year all tuition fees were eliminated and double sessions were begun, there were dramatic increases in enrollment (see Table 2.3); and in 1973 the more than 65,000 students enrolled, together with an additional 26,000 in private schools, brought matriculation in the Third Cycle up to 34 percent of the eligible population. The ability of the system to retain students was also enhanced: of those who entered the seventh grade in 1970, for example, nearly 91 percent were enrolled in the ninth grade in 1972.[4] This figure may prove somewhat higher than the future retention rate (only 85 percent of the 1971

[4] These are not refined dropout figures, since ninth-grade enrollments included repeaters and others who may not have been students in seventh grade two years previously, and excluded students who entered with the proper seventh-grade cohort but required more than the usual two years to finish the Third Cycle.

TABLE 2.3
Enrollment and Retention in Grades 7-9 of
Public Schools, 1966-73

Year	Total enrollment, gds. 7–9	Percent of gd. 6 entering gd. 7[a]	Percent of gd. 7 going on to gd. 9[b]
1966	21,665	—	—
1967	22,977	34.2%	—
1968[c]	19,104	—	—
1969	25,509	33.1	68%
1970	28,104	30.8	—
1971	39,117	46.1	79
1972	52,105	57.4	91
1973	65,390	—	—

SOURCE: ODEPOR, *Plan Quinquenal,* Cuadro 2.
   [a] Number entering grade 7 as a percentage of number enrolled in grade 6 the previous year.
   [b] Number entering grade 9 as a percentage of number enrolled in grade 7 two years previously.
   [c] There was a major teachers' strike in 1968, and the data collected that year are inconsistent with other information. Calculations dependent on these figures have been omitted from the table, along with some other unsatisfactory estimates.

seventh-graders were registered in eighth grade in 1972), but there was unquestionably a sharp rise in retention under the Reform.

The elimination of tuition was undoubtedly one reason for the increased retention rate under the Reform. No longer were parents forced to pay the monthly fees and the incidental expenses for uniforms and examinations that had been required under the old system. Moreover, early in the Reform the Ministry may have passed the word to school directors and teachers that more students were expected to pass than had done so in previous years. This policy became official in 1971, when the Ministry introduced a system of "oriented promotion" whereby students were automatically promoted unless they showed severe deficiencies in both attendance and performance. The new system also emphasized a continuous, systematic, and varied evaluation of the students throughout the nine years of basic education. The previous promotion system had been based on a single end-of-year written examination that was heavily dependent on rote memorization. A high percentage of the students customarily failed this and were forced to drop out or to repeat an entire school year. This "do or die" approach was now supposed to give way to a series of shorter tests and classroom evaluation by teachers, conducted over the entire school year.

Curriculum Reform

The Salvadoreans realized that if television were to be effective in upgrading the quality of instruction, the broadcast lessons would have to accompany a reformed curriculum. In Minister Béneke's words: "The present curriculum is archaic and is not responsive to the real needs of life. Since television is only an instrument for implementing the curriculum, the quality of the whole educational system depends on the quality of that curriculum. The effective establishment of instructional television requires at the very least the elaboration of new and better curricula."[5]

At the time Béneke made this statement, the elementary and secondary curricula written in 1956 had the official approval of the Ministry of Education, but teachers actually used a 1958 revision of them that had very little continuity from the primary to the secondary level. One of the major goals of the Educational Reform was to rewrite the school curriculum completely from first grade through secondary school. The Ministry's Technical-Pedagogical Division was given this responsibility, and a special Curriculum Commission (composed of the Ministry division chiefs, one representative each from the business community and the national university, and the Ministry's chief UNESCO adviser) was created in 1968 to review and approve the new programs.

From the beginning, curriculum reform encountered many problems. The most important of these was deciding *how* to achieve the reform. A basic decision in this regard came from Minister Béneke, who believed that El Salvador's need for middle-level skills necessitated the extension of basic, prevocational education from six to nine years. The practical consequence of this policy was to reduce the existing Third Cycle subjects from eleven to four (math, natural science, social studies, and Spanish language arts), and to add English. Henceforth, grades 7-9 would study only general natural science;

[5] República de El Salvador, *Plan Quinquenal 1968-1972, sector educación (DT No. 659)*. Consejo Nacional de Planificación y Coordinación Economica (Conoplan). San Salvador: 1968.

the specialized study of biology, chemistry and physics would not begin until the *bachillerato* (grades 10-12). The same was true in other subjects: civics, morals, history, and geography were reduced to a single social studies course oriented toward the study of El Salvador and Central America; algebra, geometry, and trigonometry were replaced by a single modern mathematics course.

Once the subject areas were determined, there remained the problem of actually writing the new curricula. Two difficulties handicapped this effort. First, only one Salvadorean curriculum writer worked in each subject area, with the help of a USAID adviser, and thus had the difficult task of preparing an entire program of study for grades 1 through 9.[6] Second, the curriculum writers did not all share Béneke's view that the existing programs were "archaic," and they resented the fact that their opinions had never been solicited on the subject. This resentment was manifested in hostility toward the ITV Division, which the curriculum writers viewed as the instigator of the move to change the curricula.

The curriculum writers began their task in a leisurely manner. During the first half of 1968, they reviewed the existing curricula and administered a survey to classroom teachers. When August came and went and no actual curriculum writing had begun, the Director of ITV, whose teams could not start taping the seventh-grade lessons without a new curriculum, began to panic. The subject specialists on the production teams were sent to the Ministry in an effort to spur completion of at least a seventh-grade curriculum. This tactic incensed the curriculum writers, who pointed out the difficulty of beginning a complete reform with the seventh grade, rather than starting with grade 1 and moving upward. In other circumstances, the curriculum reform would most probably have proceeded as they wished; but because the Ministry was committed to beginning Third Cycle TV broadcasts in February 1969, the ITV Division urgently needed the new curriculum of the first of those grades.

The basic question of how a curriculum reform could best be accomplished was never fully answered before the demands of ITV forced the writing of the first new curricula. What emerged, how-

[6] New curricula for grades 10-12 were prepared with the assistance of El Salvador's National University.

ever, did differ in many important ways from the previous programs of study. The 1958 programs were little more than long lists of unrelated facts to be memorized, whereas the new programs emphasized understanding and applying concepts. Moreover, the new curricula went into much greater detail than the old, specifying not only the content of lessons but also the objectives to be achieved, possible classroom activities to reinforce what was taught on television, strategies for evaluating student learning, and bibliographies. The thematic content of each grade level was reduced, and the continuity between grades was vastly improved.

The entire new curriculum for grades 1-9 was completed in late 1970. During that year the relationship between ITV personnel and the Ministry curriculum writers improved greatly, although it is difficult to pinpoint the causes of this improvement. One probable reason was the relative success of each reform, in that teachers and students were highly favorable not only toward television but also toward the new programs of study.

Teacher Training

In its early planning the ETV Commission did not envision the need for any retraining of teachers beyond a brief orientation to television, since they believed that classroom teachers would serve only as monitors in the ITV system. Urged to reconsider this position by UNESCO and USAID advisers, the Commission ultimately decided on a larger role for classroom teachers. This change, together with the decision to reform the curriculum, made teacher retraining a necessity. The commitment was a costly one, involving a full year's retraining that included study of the new curricula, new teaching methodology, and various other topics in addition to proper TV utilization. And the Ministry would have to pay the salaries of teachers attending the retraining course, as well as hiring classroom substitutes for them. However, because of the relatively small number of secondary teachers in El Salvador, the planners believed the initial phase of retraining could be finished in three years. They also felt the expense would be more than compensated by the benefits of increasing the professional preparation of secondary teachers, 80 percent of whom were then certified to teach only at the primary level.

When Béneke left the ETV Commission in 1967 to become Minister of Education, he was confronted with another grave problem in the area of teacher preparation. Years of uncontrolled expansion had led to the establishment of more than 60 official and private primary normal schools, and a great many recent graduates from these had been unable to find teaching positions. Béneke closed all the primary normal schools, declaring a moratorium on primary teacher training until a new normal school of high quality could be established. He decided that all future teacher training, both primary and secondary, should be concentrated in this one new school, which could also handle the retraining program for secondary teachers. San Andrés was selected as the site of the retraining program and of all subsequent teacher training. In January 1968 Béneke appointed a director and two subdirectors for the school, and a faculty was selected from the staffs of the old normal schools.

The programs offered at San Andrés in 1968 were simply a continuation of those that had previously existed elsewhere. The primary teaching students completed their course and left at the end of 1968; the secondary teachers required an additional year's training, but they and their faculty also left at the end of 1968 to complete this at a normal school in San Salvador. The remaining San Andrés faculty then turned its full attention to the secondary retraining program. This was coordinated with the gradual expansion of ITV, so that all teachers who were to use television would have previously received retraining at San Andrés. Because ITV was to be inaugurated in 28 experimental classrooms in February 1969, the first retraining course for teachers of those classes was scheduled for the vacation period of November 1968–January 1969.

This first vacation course was well received by the 100 teachers selected, who studied teaching methodology, ITV utilization, principles of secondary education, and the new seventh-grade curricula in their subject specialties. The course also provided an opportunity for additional development of the new school's resources. New textbooks were ordered, and an Instructional Materials Center was started to control the distribution of books and other teaching materials. Closed circuit television for demonstrations and practice teaching was also inaugurated in the San Andrés practice classrooms.

Television film crews on location at a coffee finca and in a rural village

Though retaining the basic framework of the first vacation course, the subsequent full-year retraining programs were strengthened by the addition of courses in evaluation, guidance, techniques of investigation, and library science, as well as by optional offerings in home economics, fine arts, industrial arts, and music. The program introduced a number of innovations in Salvadorean teacher education: entering students were administered achievement tests in their subject specialties, so that they could be taught in relatively homogeneous groups; students' daily schedules set aside free hours during which they could study, use the library, confer with professors, or simply relax; and faculty teaching loads were reduced from 35 to 15 hours per week to encourage better preparation, more rapid correction of papers, and more interaction with individual students. To increase the quality of instruction, professors were encouraged to use advanced textbooks and other teaching aids, and they were asked to submit lesson plans to the school's academic subdirector.

By the end of 1970 over a thousand teachers had completed their retraining at San Andrés, and the school began shifting its major emphasis from secondary retraining to preservice training of both primary and secondary teachers. At the outset of the Educational Reform, San Andrés was a group of abandoned, run-down buildings. Four years later it had dormitory space for 700 students, a cafeteria that could serve 900 hot meals daily, a library with over 17,000 volumes, science laboratories, a demonstration center with closed-circuit TV, an Instructional Materials Center with a full-time staff, and a practice school that encompassed grades 1-9. Its full-time faculty grew from 23 in 1969 to 40 in 1971. Most important, the school's quality increased steadily, as did its acceptance and prestige among Salvadorean teachers.

Supervision

School supervisors in the El Salvador traditional system were simply inspectors who visited classrooms to check up on teachers and turn in reports; they were not expected to offer professional advice or positive reinforcement. The architects of the Reform wanted to establish a different kind of supervisor who could advise classroom teachers and help them adapt to the problems of teaching with television and with new curricula. A first step in this direction was taken in 1967, when a "utilization section" was formed within the ITV Division.

The Utilization Section was formed chiefly to help classroom teachers adjust to television and to provide feedback to the production teams. These goals involved a number of tasks in the first year. The first was to oversee the remodeling of the 28 classrooms that had been selected by the Ministry to participate in the pilot year of television. This typically involved improving a classroom's acoustics and providing secure doors and windows as protection against thieves. The Utilization Section checked constantly to make sure that the repairs would be completed in time to get television receivers into all the classrooms before the beginning of school in February 1969. A second task involved public relations. The head of Utilization and his assistant spoke to many teacher and parent groups about the merits and potential benefits of the television system. Many parents had the notion that television would damage their children's eyes, and had to be reassured by these sessions.

Finally, the Section had the task of preparing and teaching the course on television utilization that was part of the first retraining program at San Andrés. This included a variety of basic information: where in a classroom to place a TV set for best viewing; how to adjust the set, and how and where to report sets needing repairs; the structure and use of teachers' guides and student workbooks; and how to use several different kinds of audiovisual aids. The course stressed the importance of the classroom teacher in the ITV program, helping to reassure the many teachers who had feared that television would replace them or reduce their significance in the classroom. It was stressed that ITV was simply a means of presenting material otherwise inaccessible to classroom teachers, and that teleteachers and classroom teachers were partners in the educational process.

In 1969 the Utilization Section was asked to undertake the additional tasks of supervising television classrooms and distributing guides and workbooks. The extra staff required for these activities came from graduates of the first retraining course at San Andrés. Twelve outstanding students were given special training in supervi-

sion, and six of these were finally chosen as the first classroom supervisors. This process of selection and training placed the new supervisors at an unintended disadvantage: the classroom teachers who
had been their schoolmates at San Andrés were not at all convinced
that the supervisors knew more than they did about using television.

During 1969, however, the utilization supervisors established generally good relations in the schools. Weekly visits were made to all
TV classrooms and weekly résumés of teachers' reactions to programs, guides, and workbooks were prepared for the production
teams. Unfortunately, the teams came to regard these résumés as
personal attacks by the Utilization Section instead of constructive
criticism from the field. To overcome charges that the résumés were
too subjective, the ITV Evaluation Section drew up a standard form
for teacher evaluation of programs, guides, and workbooks. The
form was distributed and collected by utilization supervisors, but
the results were tabulated and given to the production teams by the
Evaluation Section.

Anticipating the planned expansion of the ITV system, the Utilization Section began to expand and modify its own functions in
1969. Inspecting classrooms and overseeing TV repairs became the
full-time job of one member of the Section. Then, because the introduction of television into many new classrooms required increasingly
complex arrangements for distributing guides and workbooks, additional people were hired to work in that area. The Section's relationship to the utilization course at San Andrés also changed. The normal school hired two full-time teachers for the utilization course,
and formal jurisdiction for the program passed from the Utilization
Section to the San Andrés Department of Education.

Although ITV classrooms were visited weekly in 1969, the supervisors usually did no more than passively observe teachers and offer
suggestions for improvement during the breaks between classes. For
1970 the Utilization Section planned a number of changes: establishing specific goals for utilization supervision; developing a general
plan of work; preplanning school visits; establishing criteria by
which to assess both teachers' *and* supervisors' work; and extending the supervisors' duties beyond simple observation. Before these
plans could be carried out, however, an organizational shake-up

completely altered the role of the supervisors. In December 1969 Minister Béneke transferred Utilization from the ITV Division to the Division of Secondary Education. The problem was overlapping authority: since Secondary Education and ITV each employed supervisors, after the TV system had expanded to all classrooms in grades 1-9 there would have been two independent sets of supervisors covering the same schools.

The absorption of the Utilization people into the regular supervisory system of the Ministry forced a complete change in their work. Under the ITV Division they had not been called upon to solve administrative and personnel problems in the schools; but this would no longer be true. Moreover, the former ITV employees, like those already working under Secondary Education, would now have to inspect both TV and non-TV classrooms. To make matters worse, Ministry officials were unable to provide new personnel in sufficient numbers. For legal and political reasons, one entire class of new supervisors was returned to classroom teaching in the spring of 1970, rather than being assigned to the job for which they had been recruited and trained. As a consequence, during most of the year more than 900 secondary teachers were overseen by only ten supervisors. Whatever might have been accomplished by even this small staff was nullified by a clash of philosophies between the two groups that had merged. The leaders of Secondary Education and the regular supervisors viewed supervision as an administrative activity in which supervisors were primarily fiscal officers and inspectors; the ITV veterans wished to reduce administrative duties so that they could act as consultants and help solve practical teaching problems. The ITV view certainly reflected the goals for supervision established in the Ministry's Five-Year Plan; but it was not the view of the Secondary Education directors.

In December 1970, the Ministry underwent a major reorganization that removed grades 7-9 from the jurisdiction of Secondary Education and merged them with primary grades 1-6 to form a new Division of Basic Education. The former head of the ITV Utilization Section was rehired as Subdirector of Supervision for this new division, and the majority of the secondary supervisors were transferred to it to supervise grades 7-9.

This change presented an abundance of new problems. The new Subdirector of Supervision was put in charge of 100 primary supervisors, 11 Third Cycle supervisors, and 9 "itinerant" supervisors (regional leaders). To organize so many people was a difficult job. During the spring of 1971, all 120 supervisors stopped visiting schools in order to attend orientation sessions and to write various plans for the year's work. In 1970, a lack of planning had rendered supervision chaotic and inefficient; in 1971, ironically, it was still ineffective, but this time the cause was too much planning. Finally, there was a lengthy teachers' strike in 1971, and supervisors were asked to keep records of nonstriking teachers, an activity that only reinforced the teachers' image of supervisors as self-important policemen.

In retrospect, Minister Béneke's goal of making supervision "the base on which the Educational Reform rests" was not realized during the initial Five-Year Plan. The abortive program of ITV supervision, with its emphasis on helping teachers solve classroom problems, was a step in the right direction. The spirit of that effort did not disappear completely, but its application in overall school supervision proved to be a difficult and slow process.

The Role of Foreign Advisers

Although they adhered in general to the principle of local control in all areas of their Reform, the Salvadoreans received technical assistance from some 60 foreign advisers, representing a number of countries and international agencies. The advisers were instrumental in getting the reform programs under way, but their contributions varied markedly. Despite the intentions of Ministry leaders and their counterparts in the aid agencies, the effectiveness of far too many foreign advisers remained a matter of chance. Some of the best-qualified individuals, with wide experience in other countries, fared poorly, whereas others far less experienced made major contributions to the development of one or more of the reform programs. In reviewing the difficulties encountered by foreign advisers in El Salvador, one lesson emerged: the better defined an adviser's job, the more likely he was to be successful. This truth was reflected in the relative contributions made by advisers who worked in the ITV system and in the teacher retraining program as opposed to those who worked in the more culturally and politically sensitive areas of curriculum reform and school supervision.

Customarily, an adviser was not requested from a foreign agency until a particular need had been identified by the Salvadorean government; but the task of assessing needs was not handled properly at the outset of the Reform, and Ministry officials agreed to accept foreign assistance in many areas without really understanding its necessity or rationale. The burden of defining technical assistance needs often fell by default upon the aid agencies, which specified job requirements and recruited personnel. And because the bulk of the foreign advisers were paid out of grant funds, the Salvadoreans rarely challenged the agencies' judgments or the appropriateness of the advisers who were eventually recruited.

In most instances, the advisers themselves had to define their own jobs and, in a sense, to legitimize their presence in El Salvador. To this end, the ability to communicate well in Spanish was essential, and advisers who spoke the language fluently had a definite advantage. Empathy with Salvadoreans and their culture, as well as flexibility in the exercise of one's job—two highly intangible qualities—also distinguished the more successful advisers. Technical expertise and experience, though given great weight in recruiting advisers, did not seem in retrospect to count for so much as the basic ability to work well with Salvadoreans.

A revealing and rather harsh assessment of foreign technical assistance was rendered by the Salvadorean government in 1972, when the budget for foreign advisers passed directly into Salvadorean hands for the first time. At that point, the government balked at the notion of spending its own money to support foreign advisers—especially North Americans, who customarily commanded large salaries, cost-of-living allowances, and other benefits. For the first time, the cost-effectiveness of foreign technical assistance was questioned by a number of Ministry planners who believed that the country's money might better be spent on new school buildings or additional television receivers and equipment. Eventually, the Salvadorean government did hire additional foreign advisers; but it had made the point that such assistance would be more critically evaluated than in the past.

Another form of foreign-financed technical assistance involved sending Salvadoreans abroad for specialized training. In the first five years of the Reform, more than 30 Salvadoreans took advantage of such opportunities. The training programs, sponsored by a number of international agencies and foundations, ranged from short seminars in neighboring Guatemala to full-year scholarships in Europe or the United States. The value of this training was hard to judge, both for the recipients themselves and for the groups that sponsored them. Benefits seemed to vary with the applicability of the training experience to specific Reform needs and with the capabilities of the participants. The majority of the trainees unquestionably profited from their experiences abroad, but many questioned afterward whether this training had really prepared them to do their jobs any better than before.

EVALUATION AND REVISION OF ITV'S OBJECTIVES

As the Educational Reform progressed, the problems of establishing ITV and gaining acceptance for it receded, and the new concerns of coordination and quality control emerged. Accordingly, ITV's original role as catalyst of the Reform shifted subtly to one of consolidator. After the adoption of new curricula in grades 7-9 and the return of hundreds of retrained teachers to their classrooms, ITV helped to solidify change and to maintain the improved quality of classroom instruction. Nevertheless, the pressures of setting so many reforms in motion and of producing so many television series had left little time for evaluation. In the fourth year of the Reform (1971), attention focused for the first time on the role of research and feedback in the improvement of television's performance and the adjustment of its goals.

The perceived need for better information from the field was coupled with some criticism within the ITV Division of the evaluation conducted by Stanford University's Institute for Communication Research from September 1968 through December 1971. Complaints were also raised within the Ministry that too little attention had been paid to elements of the Reform beyond ITV, and that the information gathered had not been particularly useful to Salvadorean decision-makers. Two steps were taken to correct these problems: a new evaluation unit was formed in the Ministry of Education to study all aspects of the Reform; and the ITV Division's own evaluation team began to pay more attention to formative evaluation and feedback. Although the Ministry evaluation unit soon broke down because of inadequate staffing, ITV's evaluators made considerable progress in the pretesting of television lessons, the collecting of feedback from sample classrooms, and a general sensitizing of ITV personnel to the practical value of research data from the field. In time, the producers' fears of criticism receded as they gained information that seemed useful in the performance of their jobs.

At higher administrative levels in the Ministry of Education, questions arose concerning the future course of the Reform itself. The first years demonstrated that many elements of the school system could be altered simultaneously, but the long-range benefits of these changes were still in doubt. Doubts were also expressed regarding the cost-effectiveness of the ITV system. Despite these questions, plans were made to extend learning opportunities outside school and to use television more extensively in primary education and teacher training. To both foreign and domestic observers, El Salvador appeared to be risking the quality of its existing programs by expanding into so many new areas at once.

The emergence of a new planning office within the Ministry restored some faith that expansion priorities would be established in a realistic way. Although the planning office at first resisted USAID's suggestion that a thorough sector analysis precede any additional capital assistance, the idea was eventually accepted; and for the first time collaboration with other ministries was sought in order to define an educational program that would be in accord with El Salvador's overall development goals.

CHAPTER THREE

Learning with Television

A primary goal of El Salvador's Educational Reform was to encourage critical thinking among students. Minister Béneke spoke disparagingly of the "human archives" the old system had produced. The new, reformed system was to change that: future ninth-grade graduates would be prepared to adjust to a changing society and to solve its problems in more creative ways. They would also be trained to work in a variety of new industries that the Reform's planners hoped would be attracted to El Salvador by the existence of a large, well-trained labor pool.

The Stanford research team used a number of strategies to evaluate student learning under the Reform. The first involved tests of the students' basic abilities to read and learn. Little was known at the outset of the Reform about how these abilities were distributed among El Salvador's school population. Did rural children read as well and learn as readily as urban children? Were there significant differences by sex, parental education, father's occupation, socioeconomic position, and so forth? Were these differences sufficient to suggest special treatment or to warrant special learning materials for one group or another? Were the new curricula and the televised lessons effective for all ability groups, or did they serve some children better than others? Because we administered the ability tests to students throughout grades 7-9, it was possible to determine whether ITV and the other Reform programs could raise ability levels generally, and whether they helped to equalize the scores of advantaged and disadvantaged students.

A second goal was to determine whether students were learning what they were expected to learn from ITV and the new curricula. Inasmuch as there were no standardized achievement tests in El Salvador, new tests had to be built on the intended objectives of the courses. Only in this way was it possible to say how much students had learned in each course and to compare the performance of television classes with those of traditional classes and of Reform classes without television.

On the ability and reading tests we considered *who* had learned. Did students from more privileged backgrounds learn more than students from less privileged ones, urban pupils more than rural, or boys more than girls? If so, what were the implications for the curriculum and for the televised lessons? To answer these questions, all the scores were analyzed in relation to demographic and social indicators. As our evaluation of achievement extended into its third and fourth years, it was possible to ask whether ITV and the other Reform programs had had any cumulative effect on learning. To the extent that the courses were comparable from one year to the next, it was also possible to ascertain which courses were being taught more effectively or less effectively than before. And after several years of testing, it was possible to examine the effects of the Reform on the relative achievement levels of different ability groups.

THE EVALUATION DESIGN

In our evaluation of student learning, the desirability of maintaining strict scientific controls was counterbalanced by the need to conduct research in a field setting. Ideally, the research would have compared several instructional strategies (ITV, face-to-face teaching, radio, computer-managed instruction, etc.). In El Salvador, however, the crucial decision to use television had been made well before the start of our evaluation, and the country's leaders had no desire to experiment with other technologies or instructional strategies. We would also have liked to have had students and teachers assigned randomly to ITV and non-ITV classrooms, and to have isolated the particular contribution of ITV to the Reform through various experiments. But a school system is not a laboratory, and experimental considerations were hardly important to Salvadorean administrators who already had their hands full trying to implement a number of reforms simultaneously.

Under ideal circumstances, the characteristics of a population under study should resemble as closely as possible the characteristics of any other population to which the researcher wishes to generalize his findings. But El Salvador, like any other country, is unique in many ways. The concentration of her population, the centralized control of her educational system, and the strong leadership of Walter Béneke as Minister of Education are all special factors that limit the generalizations about ITV or educational reform that can be drawn from the Salvadorean experience.

On a regular basis from 1969 through 1972, a joint team of researchers from El Salvador and from Stanford University administered general ability, reading, and achievement tests, as well as survey questionnaires, to three samples of Salvadorean students. The first sample of 902 students (Cohort A) entered seventh grade in 1969. Of the 38 classrooms they attended, 25 (with a total of 581 students) were completely under the Reform, with retrained teachers, the new curriculum, teaching guides, student workbooks, and ITV. Four classrooms (with 114 students) had all the Reform elements except ITV.[1] The nine remaining classrooms (with 207 students) were "traditional." The Cohort A classrooms with ITV had been chosen for the pilot year by the Ministry of Education and thus

---

[1] The evaluation team attempted field experiments in 1969 and 1970, randomly dividing students from a few schools between classrooms with all Reform elements and classrooms with all elements except ITV. In the 1969 effort, a failure of the randomization procedure undermined the validity of the experiment, whereas administrative difficulties affected the comparisons in 1970. However, the most damaging limitation of these experiments was their lack of true control. Teachers often taught in both the ITV and non-ITV classes in a given school; thus a teacher's abilities probably accounted for learning similarities between those two classes. The teachers also mediated the effect of television on non-ITV classes. The planners of the Educational Reform had expected that one of ITV's major effects on students would be indirect, as teachers improved their own teaching both by following the structure imposed by the ITV program schedule and by using the television teachers as pedagogical models. In addition, children from ITV classes and non-ITV classes in the same school no doubt did their homework together, and probably reviewed for tests together. Thus schools were affected by the presence of ITV whether every class received ITV programs or not. Even if random assignment had been successful, and administrative difficulties nonexistent, assessment of the effects of ITV through a comparison of classes within the same school would be questionable.

were not a random sample of the school population. The "traditional" schools, however, were randomly selected by the researchers from the remaining public schools in the TV coverage area (about 75 percent of the national territory). Each sample contained students from both rural and urban schools.

Cohort B included 29 classrooms with 707 students who entered seventh grade in 1970. Because virtually all elements of the Reform were operating by 1970, the difference between instructional groups in Cohort B was solely the presence or absence of television in a classroom; and the sample included 18 classes with ITV and 11 without, with respective enrollments of 482 and 225 students.

Cohort C, entering seventh grade in 1971, included 600 pupils from 23 Reform classrooms, 18 with ITV (467 students) and 5 without (133 students). The classrooms for Cohort C were selected randomly from the schools in the Cohort A and B samples.

To be included in the final samples for Cohorts A, B, and C, students had to have taken most of our learning tests and survey questionnaires, and to have remained in the same class for two years (Cohort C) or three years (Cohorts A and B). These requirements considerably reduced the number of students in the final samples. In addition several classrooms originally included in the cohorts had to be eliminated for administrative reasons. Wherever possible, our classroom samples were selected randomly, although this was not always possible. Inevitably, there remained certain imperfections in the design of the study.

Among the most valuable procedures by which social scientists can reduce the chance for mistaken inference is the collection of panel data (i.e. studying the same individuals over a period of time) and the application of appropriate analysis models. In El Salvador, the collection of panel data permitted a much more thorough examination of the effects of ITV on a school system than had been possible in earlier studies. Ordinarily, ITV evaluations have not considered longer-range trends and effects, and learning tests or survey questionnaires have only rarely been administered more than once.[2]

[2] Cf. G. Chu and W. Schramm, *Learning from television* (Washington, D.C.: National Association of Educational Broadcasters, 1967); D. Jamison, P. Suppes, and S. Wells, *The effectiveness of alternative instructional media: A survey* (Stanford, Calif.: Institute for Communication Research, March 1973).

In contrast, the El Salvador research followed two samples of students for three years and one sample for two years. This allowed long-term comparisons between ITV and non-ITV classes, as well as a replication of these comparisons across all three cohorts. In total, patterns of student learning and attitudes were examined for eight school years (three each for Cohorts A and B, two for Cohort C), and as a result inferences from them are more valid than inferences based on measures from a single year.

PROFILE OF THREE STUDENT COHORTS

Although the cohorts were not drawn strictly at random, they were generally representative of El Salvador's postprimary student population. Historically, all postprimary students in the country have been atypical of their age group. According to the Ministry of Education, before the Reform only one out of four students who entered the first grade actually completed the six-year primary cycle and fewer than one in five customarily entered the seventh grade. There were many reasons for this high attrition rate, notably poverty and lack of opportunity, particularly in the rural areas. To alleviate these obstacles, the Reform eliminated tuition in grades 7-9 and undertook a massive program of school construction. These policies had an immediate impact on enrollment and on the kind of students who entered the seventh grade.

Students in the three cohorts were still something of an elite among their age group, although they no longer came solely from the highest social classes, as had been true in the past. Most middle- and upper-class students continued to attend private schools, which were heavily concentrated in San Salvador and other urban centers. Many of these schools were affiliated with the Catholic Church; others were commercially run institutions that had been founded in response to overflow enrollments in the public sector and the desire of parents to obtain what they believed to be a better education for their children. The proportion of students enrolled in these schools declined with the advent of ITV and the other Reform programs.

Cohort C began seventh grade in 1971, the year tuition was eliminated and double sessions began. Seventh-grade enrollment had grown by less than 3 percent between 1969 and 1970, but in response to the new policies it increased 58 percent between 1970 and 1971. A number of changes in student background accompanied this increase in enrollment (see Table 3.1). The background differences between Cohorts B and C, for example, were noticeably greater on some variables than those between A and B. Although less than 30 percent of the students' fathers in any of the cohorts possessed a level of education equivalent to that of the students themselves, the fathers of Cohort C students were the least educated. Because El Salvador is a small, densely populated country, with ac-

TABLE 3.1
Background Information for Three Student Cohorts

Item	Cohort A (N = 902)	Cohort B (N = 707)	Cohort C (N = 600)
Age (beg. grade 7)	13.9 yr.	13.6 yr.	13.8 yr.
Sex			
Male	55.4%	56.0%	52.7%
Female	44.6	44.0	47.3
Location of school			
San Salvador	22.8	16.4	20.7
Other urban	31.6	49.8	37.0
Semirural	37.8	23.9	22.4
Rural	7.8	9.9	20.0
Father's education			
None	7.5	9.2	10.2
Some primary	36.7	38.0	41.8
All primary	28.3	23.9	24.1
Some secondary	20.0	19.4	18.6
Some university	7.6	9.6	5.4
Father's occupation			
Professional	1.6	1.9	1.4
Skilled	19.7	14.6	11.1
Unskilled	78.7	83.6	87.5
Mother's education			
None	15.8	15.2	16.6
Some primary	41.2	44.4	43.3
All primary	24.9	20.6	22.9
Some secondary	16.0	16.3	15.3
Some university	2.2	3.5	1.8
Home TV ownership (Mar. 1971)	49.6	51.6	36.4
Percent of sample repeating at least one grade	47.0	47.0	43.8

NOTE: Data were rarely missing for more than 1–2 percent of the students, although for variables that were measured only once (such as repetition rates) scores were missing for up to 10 percent of the sample. In all cases, the missing scores were excluded from calculations.

tive mass media, television ownership proved to be a reliable discriminator of socioeconomic status. And in this case, too, Cohort C students were noticeably less well off.

A four-category classification of school urbanization was used in the evaluation—San Salvador, other urban, semirural, and rural. Sample schools were selected within each category so that the effects of urbanization could be studied. When demographic data from the three cohorts were analyzed along this urban/rural scale, urban students were found to be much better off than their rural counterparts. They were generally younger and had a lower repetition rate in earlier grades; their fathers and mothers had more schooling and better jobs; and they had a wider range of mass media available in the home. Many more students from San Salvador, in particular, claimed to have television sets at home. On virtually all background variables, in fact, greater differences were found between San Salvador students and students from the rest of the country than between any of the other groups on the urban/rural scale.

As El Salvador expanded school enrollments, more opportunities became available to the less advantaged, and in particular to rural students. This gave added impetus to our plan to study not only the overall quality of learning under the new system, but also the impact of the system on the various socioeconomic subgroups included in the sample.

BASIC SKILLS LEARNING

General ability and reading tests were administered repeatedly as part of our evaluation, and, as Figure 3.1 illustrates, large gains on both tests were recorded by all three student cohorts.[3] Three factors help to explain these results. The first was simply that students improved their performance on the tests because they became more familiar with them. Initially the great majority of them had had no previous experience with multiple-choice tests, and the importance of such experience is well known. In fact, the makers of standardized tests generally distribute practice versions of their tests so that students can familiarize themselves with new question-and-answer formats. These samples were not available in El Salvador, however, and

[3] See Appendix B for detailed scores.

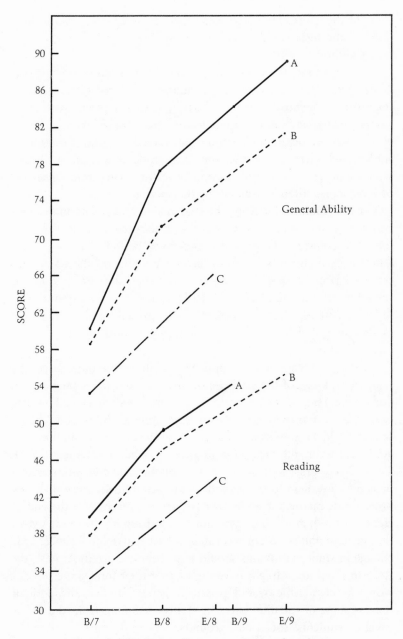

3.1. General ability and reading scores over time, by cohorts

some of the gain achieved between the first and second administrations of the tests could certainly be ascribed to an increased test-taking ability.

The second factor influencing gains on the test scores was the students' maturation. Learning opportunities unrelated to the schools (exposure to the media, visits to the city, or simply coping with one's environment) may influence intellectual growth significantly. However, since our research design did not include a control sample of students who left school after the sixth grade, it was impossible to separate the effects of simply having aged three years from the effects of having also attended school for that period.

The final factor influencing the students' improvement on the general ability and reading tests was the effect of schooling itself. Although it could not be proved that a given period of school attendance caused students to gain a certain amount on the tests, data reported later in this chapter will show that alternative kinds of schooling (traditional, Reform with ITV, and Reform without ITV) did have different effects on general ability growth; and if differences in schooling had this effect, schooling per se must also have influenced scores.

Although overall increases in general ability were quite large, the relative rankings of the students on the tests did not change much during the Third Cycle of Basic Education. Between 55 and 78 percent of the variance in the students' final general ability and reading scores could be predicted from their performance on similar tests administered at the beginning of seventh grade (see Appendix D, Table D.1). This suggests that the abilities Salvadorean students brought with them to the seventh grade determined, more than any other single factor, the ability levels they had reached by the end of eighth or ninth grade. This was not a surprising result: to the extent that general ability scores accurately reflect native intelligence, little change in student rankings should have been expected. At best, the Reform's architects might have hoped that their innovative policies would accelerate the overall growth in general ability, and perhaps redress some of the differences in ability stemming from the differences in students' social backgrounds.

Factors Influencing Basic Skills at the Beginning of Seventh Grade

Multiple regression analyses revealed that the original scores on both the general ability and the reading tests in each cohort were consistently related to three variables: sex, urbanization, and age.[4] Boys consistently outscored girls, a trend that could not be explained by any of the background variables already mentioned. If anything, girls came from more privileged backgrounds than did boys. Two general explanations for their inferior performance might be suggested. First, they may simply have been less intelligent. None of our data definitively refuted this hypothesis; but comparative data from the U.S. and other countries indicate that girls usually outperform boys in primary school, and that only at higher academic levels does the reverse occur.[5] Since this trend has never been accepted as evidence of superior female intelligence, it is unreasonable to make the opposite assumption in the Salvadorean case. More likely, the norms and self-expectations of the Salvadorean culture account for the sex difference in basic skills learning. This hypothesis was not investigated directly, but numerous conversations with students and parents corroborated it. Salvadorean families believed that education was more essential for boys than for girls; and when forced to make a choice, poor parents were more apt to keep their sons in school. Also, girls' educational aspirations were generally lower than boys', and the careers they envisioned required less schooling (see Chapter 5).

Rural children also entered seventh grade with lower scores on the tests than their urban counterparts. This was not surprising, given their poorer backgrounds and less effective primary schooling. In El Salvador, classroom teachers with the least experience are usually assigned to the countryside, and the materials and facilities in rural schools are inferior to those in urban schools. We confirmed

[4] There were positive correlations between the other control variables (parents' education and wealth) and the basic skills scores as well. However, those were not consistently maintained when all six variables were entered into the regression equation simultaneously.

[5] See E. Maccoby, ed., *The development of sex differences* (Stanford, Calif.: Stanford University Press, 1966).

these differences through visits to schools throughout the country.

Finally, age was negatively related to seventh-grade test scores (see Appendix D, Table D.2). That is, older students within a grade did worse than younger ones. This trend puzzled the evaluation team at first, given the positive effects of growing older referred to earlier; however, a closer scrutiny of the children's backgrounds explained it. A Salvadorean child who was old for his or her grade had either repeated a year of school, entered school late, or dropped out for a year or more during primary school. Each of these situations was more common among children from disadvantaged homes.

Influence of Background Variables on Change in Basic Skills

Boys, urban students, younger students in a grade, children with better-educated parents, and children from wealthier families all outperformed their peers on general ability and reading tests at the beginning of seventh grade. Given this start, what happened? Did students who began with a head start increase their initial advantage, or did the disadvantaged students gain more rapidly during the Third Cycle, closing the gap in basic skills? This question was answered by examining the influence of the background variables on the increases in general ability and reading scores that were recorded by each student cohort.[6]

Age and sex were the only variables whose influence on student gains on the general ability and reading tests was generally consistent and of large magnitude (coefficients greater than .10) across all three cohorts (see Appendix B). Boys gained more rapidly than girls, and younger children more rapidly than older children within a grade. The second trend was particularly strong in Cohort A. Was it the fact of being older in a grade, of having repeated a grade, or of having entered school late that caused some students to feel less competent than their peers and thus to achieve poorly? Or were there reasons why some pupils arrived in seventh grade later that also explained their relatively low achievement? They could have been intellectually or emotionally unprepared for primary school, or they could have come from families that required their presence in the home during part of the year. They could have been forced to repeat one or more

[6] See Appendix B.

grades because of illness, or they could have had to wait one or more years in order to transfer schools. In sum, a large number of circumstances might possibly explain the relatively low achievement of older students.

The data did not permit a separation of the two hypotheses (i.e., that age in grade alone affected student achievement, or that students' backgrounds affected *both* age in grade and achievement). However, the hypothesis attributing the major influence solely to student backgrounds was rejected, since age proved to be a more powerful predictor of change in skills than any of the background variables. If by assumption, or by additional research directed to the problem, one were able to conclude that older children will always achieve less in a particular grade, one might recommend that every effort be made to move students through the school system as smoothly as possible. El Salvador in fact inaugurated just such a policy under its Educational Reform, sharply reducing what had previously been a high repeater rate.

Another hypothesis suggested that students' basic skills scores at the beginning of seventh grade had influenced their subsequent gains on the tests. A reexamination of Figure 3.1 indicates that they did. Although complete comparisons of general ability gains were not possible, we determined that between the beginning of eighth grade and the end of ninth grade Cohort A students had increased their general ability scores by 12.3 points. During the same period Cohort B gained only 10 points. Between the beginning of seventh and the beginning of eighth grade, Cohort B increased 12.3 points, but between the beginning of seventh and the end of eighth grade, Cohort C increased only 12.6 points. Undoubtedly, Cohort B would have gained several more points in eighth grade, had we tested this. The inference that Cohort B gained more rapidly than Cohort C therefore seems justified.

In sum, Cohort A, which started highest in general ability, gained more than Cohort B, which in turn gained more than Cohort C. Why this was true is less clear. It could be that students who entered with higher general ability scores took more advantage of their schooling. Alternatively, each cohort may have received less satisfactory schooling than its predecessor. Cohort A, entering seventh grade in 1969, included the first 32 pilot television classes, which undoubtedly received special attention from teachers and administrators. Cohort C students entered seventh grade in 1971, the year enrollments were expanded dramatically. Their classes were much larger, double sessions were required to handle the overflow, and teachers were forced to take on an extra teaching load. Any of these factors could have lowered the learning of Cohort C students during the Third Cycle.

Influence of ITV and the Reform on Basic Skills Learning

In general, students in ITV classrooms gained more in general ability than did students in traditional classrooms (Cohort A) or students in Reform classrooms without ITV (Cohorts B and C).[7] There were no significant differences between gains of the comparison groups in reading. A mean change score was calculated for each subgroup of each cohort by subtracting its mean on the first administration of the general ability test from its mean on the last administration of the same test (see Appendix D, Tables D.3 and D.4). In Cohorts B and C, ITV classrooms began seventh grade with higher means on general ability and reading. To control for this, the influences of various demographic and background variables (sex, age, wealth, father's education, mother's education, and urbanization) on the change scores were estimated and then subtracted from the raw change scores, yielding residual change scores. The residual change scores on general ability, free from the influence of background factors, remained significantly in favor of the ITV classrooms. None of the reading differences were significant when either raw scores or residual scores were used.

This *post hoc* control procedure was not completely satisfying, since it was impossible to ascertain whether all the causes of the original test score differences had been adequately controlled. However, given the character of the panel data collected over four years, the superior gains of the ITV classrooms on the general ability test

[7] These comparisons of instructional systems were undertaken only between students in schools outside San Salvador. ITV and non-ITV classes were not well matched in the highly urbanized capital, and including them would have biased the comparison.

were quite convincing. The fact that the trend favoring Reform with ITV appeared in comparisons both with traditional classes and with classes having all elements of the Reform except television—including those from Cohort A in which the original advantage belonged to the traditional classrooms—was also powerful confirming evidence.

Significant differences in test scores do not necessarily provide adequate policy guidance. A decision-maker must know not only the statistical significance of such results but also their practical implications. One might ask how much gain, over and above that achieved by non-ITV classes, could be purchased by additional investment in ITV. In the event, the Salvadorean expenditure on ITV and other reforms (see Chapter 7) seems to have paid off. Our testing of ITV and non-ITV groups in the three cohorts showed the following percentage gains in general ability (over a three-year period for Cohorts A and B and a two-year period for Cohort C):[8]

Cohort A, Reform classes with ITV	54.2%
Cohort A, traditional classes	47.3
Cohort B, with ITV	42.5
Cohort B, without ITV	37.0
Cohort C, with ITV	26.4
Cohort C, without ITV	20.6

These results showed a percentage of learning advantage for ITV classes of 14.6 percent in Cohort A, 14.8 percent in Cohort B, and 28.2 percent in Cohort C (although these estimates are subject to error factors perhaps as large as 10 or 20 percent at the 95-percent confidence level).

With this evidence in hand to support the Salvadoreans' expectation that students in ITV classes would improve their basic skills more rapidly than students in non-ITV classes, a second important question arose: Did ITV reduce the gap in basic skills between ad-

[8] For purposes of this comparison, we replaced the Cohort A level 3 exam score from the beginning of the seventh grade with level 4 equivalents from Table 71, p. 60 of the test manual (Inter-American Series, published by Guidance Testing Associates, Austin, Texas): 86.99 on level 3 equals 57.0 on level 4; 88.56 on level 3 equals 58.6 on level 4. To compute the percent advantage of ITV classes, we divided the percent non-ITV gain in ability by the percent ITV gain minus the percent non-ITV gain.

vantaged and disadvantaged students? To answer this question, the three cohorts were divided once again into ITV and non-ITV subgroups; and the relative influences of age, father's education, urbanization, and the other background variables on students' gains in general ability were compared for each subgroup. (The analysis procedures are described in detail in Appendix B.)

ITV and non-ITV subsamples did not consistently differ across cohorts with regard to the influence of any of the background variables. That is not to say that for one or another cohort the influence of a given variable might not have been different. For example, as we noted earlier, older students tended to learn less than younger ones in all the cohorts; and in Cohort A this tendency was more extreme among traditional students than among ITV students: on the average, each additional year of age cost ITV students 2.4 points, whereas traditional students lost 4.2 points. If Cohort A had been the only one studied, the natural conclusion would have been that ITV opened gaps between originally advantaged younger students and disadvantaged older students less than did traditional instruction. However, this tendency did not hold up across all three cohorts. For Cohort C there was no difference between subsamples. And for Cohort B there was a very small difference, but in the opposite direction. Such inconsistent findings—and they were similar for other variables—must lead to the conclusion that instructional conditions did not mediate the influence of background variables on general ability gain.

ACHIEVEMENT LEARNING

Achievement tests in science, mathematics, and social studies were administered to the three student cohorts at the beginning and end of each school year (see Table 3.2). The Educational Testing Service of Princeton, New Jersey, constructed these for the Stanford research team in order to measure students' learning of the concepts and skills that the reformed Third Cycle curricula were intended to teach.[9]

[9] How accurately each test sampled its curriculum must remain in doubt. Between each two school years, the curriculum division of the Ministry of Education worked under great pressure to finish the curricula necessary for the following year. Usually, these were not complete until two months before the

TABLE 3.2
*Achievement Test Administration Schedule in
Math, Science, and Social Studies*

Year	Cohort A	Cohort B	Cohort C
1969	3 subject tests before & after grade 7		
1970	3 subject tests before & after grade 8	3 subject tests before & after grade 7	
1971	3 subject tests before & after grade 9	3 subject tests before & after grade 8	3 subject tests before & after grade 7
1972		3 subject tests before & after grade 9	3 subject tests before & after grade 8

Each test contained 50 multiple-choice questions. During the first two years of the Reform faulty communication between the curriculum writers and the ITV production teams delayed the preparation of both the new curricula and the accompanying tests; and at the beginning of the 1970 school year administration of the tests had to be postponed for almost three months. Because the achievement tests had to be prepared so far in advance of the television lessons, it was impossible to know beforehand how much of a given curriculum

---

school year was to begin. In order to have tests geared to each curriculum for administration at the beginning of the school year, the document was immediately mailed to the Educational Testing Service. Curriculum writers or advisers to the Ministry had generally indicated which concepts were most important. ETS then wrote a first draft of the test. When possible, questions were borrowed from tests used elsewhere; otherwise new questions were written. A Spanish version of the test was then sent back to El Salvador for review by the television production teams. Ideally, the content of the test was to be checked against the instruction the ITV team for that subject was planning for the year. Since the teams prepared not only the teleseries but also the teachers' guides and the student workbooks, they had de facto control over which parts of the curricula would in fact be emphasized and which ignored. Unfortunately, the teams themselves worked under great pressure, particularly in the early years. At best, they had two to three weeks lead time on broadcast dates. When the first drafts of the tests were made available to them, they had only a vague notion of what they would be teaching even a month hence, let alone what they would be teaching at the end of the year. Thus their review of the test was mainly concerned with whether language in the test conformed to Salvadorean usage.

would actually be covered during the school year. Moreover, it was not possible to determine whether or not the television classes' emphasis on certain concepts would be adequately reflected in the achievement tests. A much more complete content analysis of the teleclasses would have been required to resolve the problem.

In the belief that a more accurate sampling of the curricula could be obtained through direct consultation with the ITV staff, the evaluation unit itself revised the achievement tests in 1972, raising the number of questions on each test from 50 to 60. When a particular subject is taught properly, and when a test concerning that subject proves to be a reliable and valid measure of learning, test designers and teachers can expect students to answer a reasonable number of test questions (perhaps 70 percent) correctly. Of course, the objective difficulty of any test can be set arbitrarily. In the absence of advance information about the content and emphases of ITV lessons, our construction of tests for El Salvador had no satisfactory control over the degree of difficulty; hence adopting precise performance levels on end-of-year tests as criteria for achievement could not be justified. Instead, since identical tests were administered at the beginning and end of each school year as part of the evaluation, yearly gains as a percentage of beginning-of-year test scores were eventually adopted as the basic measures of student achievement. Unlike absolute gains or final test scores, percentage gains could be corrected for the differences that existed between the student subgroups and between subject areas at the beginning of the year. Because it proved useful as a cutting point in the comparisons, a 20-percent gain was set as the criterion for learning sufficiency.

The average percentage gains in our sample groups are given in Table 3.3. With one exception, there was a significant learning gain in every course each year, and in every student cohort; only in eighth-grade tests for Cohort C was the gain insignificant. Given the large number of students in each cohort, the significant gains included four that improved by less than 10 percent on the original scores. Under these circumstances, there were obviously more important questions than statistical significance: namely, was the overall learning of the students satisfactory, and did the ITV classes learn appreciably more than classes without ITV?

TABLE 3.3
Average Percentage Gains on Achievement Tests

Subject and grade	Cohort A (N = 712)	Cohort B (N = 505)	Cohort C (N = 558)
Mathematics			
Seventh	48.1%	21.7%	23.5%
Eighth	12.0	18.5	16.9
Ninth	16.4	26.0	—
Science			
Seventh	30.2	22.7	20.9
Eighth	7.4	12.3	.7
Ninth	9.9	12.6	—
Social studies			
Seventh	26.8	27.6	25.8
Eighth	10.2	12.4	20.1
Ninth	8.6	4.2	—

NOTE: For more detailed test results, see Appendix D.

Of the 24 percentage gains, 11 were greater than 20 percent, and nine of these were in the seventh grade, where all the gains topped this cutting point. In the two higher grades, only one figure for each year exceeded 20 percent. This is not quite as bad as it appears, since the small gains for Cohort A in grade 8 were somewhat misleading. Owing to the late arrival of the new eighth-grade curriculum in 1970 and the corresponding delay in test construction, the first tests for this measurement were not administered until the third month of the school year. This circumstance unquestionably limited the gains recorded, since part of the year's learning was already present in the belated "before" scores.

Distinct patterns by grade emerged when the percentage gains of the ITV and non-ITV subgroups within each cohort were compared.[10] In eight of the nine seventh-grade comparisons, ITV students gained proportionately more than their non-ITV counterparts; and every ITV gain was greater than 20 percent, whereas only two of the non-ITV gains were that large. In the next two grades the patterns were quite different: the non-ITV subgroups consistently outgained their ITV peers in science; the results in social studies were about even; and the math results favored the ITV students, with only the non-ITV subgroup of Cohort B outperforming its counterpart.

[10] See Appendix B for complete results and comparisons.

In order to systematize these comparisons, ratios of ITV to non-ITV mean scores were calculated for each student cohort and were then plotted on graphs, as in Figure 3.2. Within each graph, lines with positive slopes (from lower left to upper right) represent instances when ITV students gained more than non-ITV students; negative slopes (upper left to lower right) represent instances when non-ITV students gained more. For example, at the beginning of seventh grade the mean math scores of the ITV and non-ITV subgroups in Cohort A were 11.97 and 12.44, respectively, yielding a starting ratio of .96. At the end of the year, the ITV subgroup mean of 18.24 surpassed the non-ITV mean of 16.85, for a ratio of 1.08. The line connecting these two ratios has a positive slope.

By comparing the ratios for different years, it was possible to see if any cumulative advantages developed in achievement when ITV was used. Turning once again to the performance of Cohort A's subgroups in math, one finds that over the entire three years the mean of the ITV subgroup increased from .96 to 1.16 of the non-ITV mean. In fact, in every subject and in every cohort the cumulative change in achievement favored the ITV students; that is, the ITV to non-ITV ratio was always larger at the end of ninth grade than it was at the beginning of seventh grade.

We also compared the ITV and non-ITV subgroups according to the overall magnitude of the achievement gains they obtained in all the tests for each grade: "high" was more than 20 percent on a test; "middle" was between 10 and 20 percent; and "low" was less than 10 percent. Considering each gain score as the average improvement of a single cohort taking before-and-after tests in a single subject, the distribution of scores, high/middle/low, was:

With ITV:		*Without ITV:*	
seventh grade	9/0/0	seventh grade	2/6/1
eighth grade	1/6/2	eighth grade	2/4/3
ninth grade	2/1/3	ninth grade	2/2/2

Obviously, the students with ITV did far better than those without it in the seventh grade; but in later grades the advantages of ITV were not apparent. How can this sharp drop from overwhelming success in grade 7 to indifferent performance in grades 8 and 9 be explained?

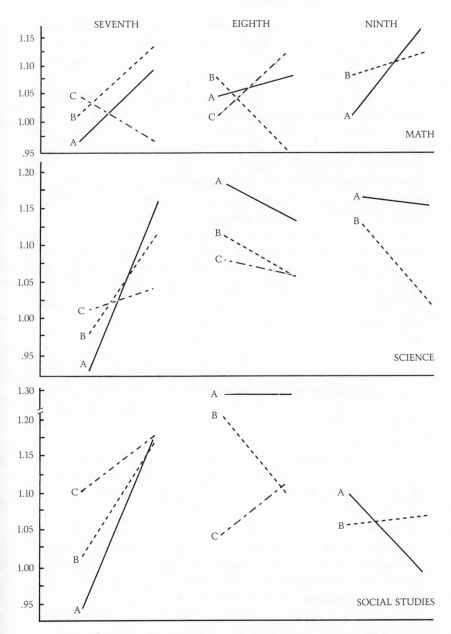

3.2. Ratio of ITV mean to non-ITV mean on achievement tests

One obvious explanation would be a novelty effect. The students first encountered televised lessons in the seventh grade, along with other elements of the Reform. It was an exciting experience to be in an ITV classroom, and one that probably enhanced the students' motivation. In contrast, students who did not receive televised instruction and its accompanying innovations may have been less motivated to learn. However, as the novelty of television wore off so did the superior learning performance of ITV students. In the final analysis, this pattern suggests that ITV's advantage may be no more than that of motivating students strongly for a short time. A parallel decline we observed in the students' own attitudes toward ITV (see Chapter 4) reinforced this interpretation.

A second explanation of the relatively poor performance of ITV students in grades 8 and 9 is that the television classes transmitted to the seventh grade were generally higher in quality. The production teams that made the initial series of seventh-grade lessons in 1969 had received the best training. In 1970, new teams with only a minimum of training were assigned to make the first programs for the eighth grade; meanwhile, the experienced teams were allowed to revise their seventh-grade series. In 1971, the original seventh-grade teams were put to work on the first ninth-grade series; but their work was interrupted midway through the school year by a teachers' strike that disrupted the entire school system, and broadcasting of the ninth-grade series was not resumed for the remainder of the school year.

In 1972, ITV instruction in grades 8 and 9 improved somewhat. As a result, in eighth-grade social studies and eighth- and ninth-grade math the ITV subgroups not only outgained the non-ITV subgroups but also achieved 20-percent gains. If the novelty effect of television was the only factor influencing the earlier learning successes, the 1972 results should not have occurred. But it would seem that although the novelty effect no doubt helped ITV classes in grade 7, the superior quality of the telelessons they received was just as important. In later grades, the students received inferior programs, and they missed many lessons because of the strike. The negative effects of these factors were most apparent in science and least apparent in math.

It was ironic, in fact, that science proved to be the least successful ITV series in terms of student learning. The early advocates and planners of El Salvador's ITV system had claimed that one of class-room television's greatest assets would be the students' exposure to lab experiments and demonstrations that had formerly been available only in the exclusive private schools of San Salvador. The fact that students in ITV science classes never obtained end-of-year scores more than 11 percent greater than their beginning-of-year scores suggests that the ITV science series, experiments and all, fell far short of the planners' expectations.

PATTERNS OF CLASSROOM LEARNING

Research results from many countries have documented the important influence of social class and other background variables on student achievement in school. Some scholars have concluded that the influence of background is in fact so strong that it overshadows the effect of most educational reforms and innovations. Reform programs have rarely reduced the learning gaps between advantaged and disadvantaged students; and they may even have widened these gaps, since innovations have tended to reach only the most modern "model" schools. But even though they admit that most reform programs in the past have been unevenly distributed and have not appreciably improved learning, educational planners throughout the world still believe that investment in the right resources and reforms can make a profound difference in the learning of students, particularly disadvantaged students.

We have argued that student background characteristics and later schooling both influenced learning in important ways in El Salvador. The influence of sex, age in grade, and the like on the students' general ability and reading scores at the beginning of seventh grade was apparent, as was the particularly strong influence of a student's sex and age on changes in those scores. Enrollment in an ITV class also exerted a powerful influence on learning. Our analysis focused on individual students and their backgrounds. However, many characteristics are shared by entire classrooms of students—the economic and social background of a community, the characteristics of a particular school, and peer-group influences, for example. To clarify the importance of these variables, we shall now reconsider some of the conclusions reached earlier, this time using the classroom instead of the individual student as our unit of analysis.

Because of the high repeater rates in Salvadorean primary grades before the Reform, the ages of students in a Third Cycle classroom varied widely at the time of the study

School and community data were gathered from public records and from interviews with school directors and community officials in the spring of 1971 (the questionnaire used in this study is reproduced in Appendix C). Learning data were taken exclusively from Cohort B students. Only 29 classrooms were included in that cohort; as a result, correlation coefficients based on those classrooms were subject to a large error. The coefficients obtained were high enough to justify certain interpretations and conclusions, but the small sample limited the use of regression analyses.

For each of the communities in which a sample school was located, we collected information on a variety of subjects. To facilitate analysis, this was consolidated in three scales: availability of education, ease of access to a city, and overall community affluence.

The education scale was based on opportunities for schooling beyond grade 9. Fifteen of the 29 communities in the sample had schools offering the *bachillerato* (high school) or *carrera corta* (business course) degrees. Another eight were located within daily commuting distance of such institutions. In only six communities would the students have been forced to leave home in order to continue their education. Ease of access to a city, the second scale, was based on the time needed to travel by bus to the nearest metropolitan center. El Salvador has regular, if uncomfortable, bus service throughout the country; and as it turned out, not one of the communities in the sample was more than two hours from a city or more than three-and-a-half hours from the capital. Also, there was daily bus service to a city from each of the communities. Rural Salvadoreans are not nearly as isolated as rural people in most other Latin American countries, who must often travel for days to reach an urban center. This scale, though it showed little variation in itself, proved to be highly correlated with other student, school, and community characteristics. The scale measuring community affluence was formed by combining five variables: presence of a bank; number of public telephones per thousand population; number of paved streets; number of newspapers sold per thousand population; and presence of a factory employing more than 50 persons.[11]

Four other indices were constructed from information about the schools themselves. The first was based on number of Third Cycle students enrolled. Eleven of the 29 schools had 500 or more students, nine had between 100 and 200, and four had fewer than 100. The second index broadly classified a school's physical condition as good (4 schools), bad (3), or average (22). For the third index, school directors were asked if their schools had certain facilities: a faculty library (10 schools), a student library (9), a science laboratory (5), inside plumbing (28), space for recess activities (20), an open field for physical education (12), an auditorium (8), a telephone (14), and a mimeograph machine (27). The eventual index used only three of these variables: faculty library, telephone, and mimeograph machine. On the final index, we rated the adequacy of a school's teaching materials, using a point score derived from responses to questions about the availability of specific teaching aids.

The peer background variables analyzed in the study of community and school effects were selected from those used in the earlier analysis of individual students: home TV ownership during the years of the study, father's and mother's education, age, and percentage of repeaters in a classroom. Each class was assigned the mean score of all its members on these variables.

Scores on the two basic skills tests (general ability and reading) and on the achievement tests in math, science, and social studies

[11] The weights for each variable in this wealth scale were determined by their loadings on the principal factor of a factor analysis.

were combined to form a cognitive skills index for each Cohort B classroom. We calculated this index for each class three times: beginning of grade 7, beginning of grade 8, and end of grade 9.

By reanalyzing the learning data from the perspective of the classroom rather than the individual student, we were attempting to determine the relative influence of three kinds of variables: community, school, and student background. The results (see Appendix Table D.11) were what one might expect. All three variables were closely related: children from the highest socioeconomic strata usually lived in urban areas, attended the best equipped schools, and made the highest scores on the cognitive skills indices; rural students were located at the opposite extremes on the same variables. In the country teaching materials were less likely to be adequate, the physical condition of the school was likely to be poorer, and the facilities were fewer. Teacher quality was not evaluated as part of this survey, but other evidence indicated that this resource was also distributed unevenly. City schools were considered more attractive places to work than were rural ones, and teachers with seniority and superior training generally gravitated to them.

The relation of contextual and background variables to cognitive skills was particularly striking. Altogether, 75 percent of the variance (multiple correlation squared) in cognitive skills at the beginning of seventh grade could be predicted from the community, peer, and school variables. Clearly, when Salvadorean students arrived in seventh grade, what they knew and the skills they possessed were profoundly affected by their backgrounds. Since the skills with which students left the Third Cycle were closely related to those with which they entered, approximately 66 percent of the variance in their cognitive skills at the end of ninth grade could be predicted from the same variables.[12] However, the drop in predictability does suggest that the *change* in cognitive skills during Third Cycle was not positively related to student background or school characteristics. Although the influence of background factors remained strong, three

[12] Multiple correlation coefficients were calculated to summarize the importance of the community, school, and peer variables in predicting cognitive skills. The squares of these coefficients indicated what percentage of the variance in the cognitive skills indices could be predicted from these characteristics.

years of schooling may have reduced it; and ITV, the first educational resource to be distributed universally (and thus equally) in El Salvador, may have been a major factor in this change.

THE INFLUENCE OF ITV ON CLASSROOM LEARNING

We have seen that in all three cohorts the presence of ITV in a classroom was positively related to a student's percentage gain in general ability. This was confirmed when we reanalyzed this finding as well, again using Cohort B alone and taking classrooms as the basic units. As in earlier analyses, it was necessary to eliminate the three ITV classrooms located in San Salvador because there were no comparable non-ITV classrooms to balance them. The remaining 26 classrooms (15 with ITV, 11 without) were ranked according to the averages of their scores on the cognitive index at the beginning of grade 7 and at the end of grade 9, with the highest mean ranked as 1 and the lowest as 26.

At the beginning of seventh grade, the ITV and non-ITV subsamples had essentially identical mean ranks—13.53 and 13.45, respectively—indicating that the assignment of ITV to a class was unrelated to cognitive skills. By the end of the Third Cycle the situation had completely changed. The mean rank of the ITV classes rose to 10.07, whereas that of the non-ITV classes fell to 18.18. Considering that the highest mean rank the 15 ITV classrooms could have attained was 8.0 (if they had occupied ranks 1-15), and that the lowest mean rank the 11 non-ITV classrooms could have obtained was 21 (by occupying ranks 16-26), the change that did occur was quite large (it is significant at $p < .02$ on the Mann-Whitney U Test). From another perspective, 11 of the 15 ITV classrooms, or 73 percent, moved up in rank between the beginning and end of the Third Cycle; but only 2 of the 11 non-ITV classrooms (18 percent) improved their rank.

Thus ITV's influence was even more impressive when viewed from the perspective of the classroom than it had appeared to be when the sampling unit was the individual student. In fact, there was no other community, school, or background variable that had as strong a correlation with change in cognitive skills (see Appendix Table D.12).

SUMMARY AND IMPLICATIONS

On a regular basis from 1969 through 1972, general ability and reading tests, as well as mathematics, science, and social studies achievement tests, were administered to three cohorts of students. Cohort A, entering seventh grade in 1969, included students studying with television and other elements of the Educational Reform as well as students studying in the traditional way. Cohorts B and C, which started seventh grade in 1970 and 1971, respectively, included only students from Reform classes, although these groups were divided into ITV and non-ITV subsamples.

ITV and the other Reform measures were successful in enhancing student learning. On most learning comparisons, students exposed to ITV, retrained teachers, the revised curricula, and new learning materials outperformed their peers in traditional classes and in classes that had all elements of the Reform except television.

In all three cohorts, the ITV students gained from 15 to 25 percent more on the general ability tests than did their non-ITV peers during Third Cycle. The advantage was not diminished when controls for socioeconomic status and for individual student characteristics were applied. On reading tests, ITV and non-ITV students gained about the same. ITV students in each cohort also gained more than non-ITV students on the achievement tests administered in seventh grade. The ITV advantage in mathematics was maintained through ninth grade. In social studies, eighth- and ninth-grade achievement results were mixed: sometimes ITV students gained more, sometimes non-ITV students gained more. In science, non-ITV students gained more in both upper grades.

Older children within each cohort (those who had started school late, repeated a grade, or otherwise interrupted their education) gained less on the basic skills tests than did younger children. Also, boys gained more than girls. However, both age and sex, as well as father's education, family wealth and urbanization, were positively related to the students' initial scores on the basic skills tests taken at the beginning of grade 7. Television and the other Reform programs did not consistently lessen the influence of these variables on basic skills test performance.

Finally, to double-check the learning results based on student test scores and to investigate further the influence of community, school, and student background characteristics on learning, we posed additional questions using the classrooms rather than the individual student as the unit of analysis. The results of these additional analyses confirmed the trends we had noted for individuals.

At the outset of her Educational Reform, El Salvador ran the risk of increasing existing inequalities by instituting new programs that might prove to affect only the best schools. Not only did the large urban schools already have the best facilities and teaching materials, but they tended to enroll a much higher percentage of students from the more advantaged social groups. Poorer students, who were the least able intellectually and financially to succeed in postprimary education, were most often enrolled in ill-equipped and understaffed schools. Fortunately, the Reform programs, and especially ITV, managed to break with this tradition of unequally distributed educational resources. Although the most experienced and best educated teachers continued to work in the richer urban schools, all schools received retrained teachers, a revised curriculum, and new learning materials. Of greatest importance, however, was the fact that by 1973 television lessons were reaching at least 70 percent of all Third Cycle students in El Salvador.

Learning was influenced strongly by student background variables such as family wealth and level of parents' education, and somewhat less strongly by school and community variables. But ITV, always introduced in the context of the overall Reform, was more important than any other community or classroom variable in predicting student learning. In contrast to the rather disappointing results of educational innovation in other countries, El Salvador's investment in ITV and related reform programs did appear to make a major difference in what students actually learned.

The learning advantage of the Reform classrooms with ITV over traditional classrooms (Cohort A only) was roughly equivalent to their advantage over classrooms without ITV (Cohorts B and C). Can one therefore assume that if the Reform programs had not included ITV, they would not have produced learning gains significantly greater than those of the traditional system? Conversely, would ITV alone have led to increased learning?

We believe that the various non-ITV programs, though according to our results they were not decisive in themselves, were essential to ITV's success. The year's retraining that all teachers received unquestionably improved their effective use of the television lessons. So did the student workbooks and teaching guides, which strongly reinforced the television lessons. When the television schedule was interrupted for some reason, or when a sloppily taught telelesson proved confusing to students, these supplementary materials provided an alternative source from which essential concepts could be learned. In short, television did not prove to be the intrusion it might have been had ITV been introduced without complementary reforms, as had been the case in most other countries.

The most impressive gains in learning under the Reform-ITV system were on the general ability tests. Educational planners often hope that the instructional innovations they adopt will not only increase learning in specific subject areas but also improve the students' general intellectual skills. In El Salvador, students gained both on individual subject tests and on the tests of numerical, verbal, and nonverbal reasoning abilities. However, there was no apparent improvement in reading skills. It would seem that El Salvador's educational planners still have to make fundamental changes in both the Spanish curriculum and the Spanish teleseries itself.

Finally, despite the overall evidence in favor of the ITV classrooms, the adequacy of television's achievement in specific courses must be questioned. Only in seventh grade did Salvadorean students consistently improve their knowledge of a subject by as much as 20 percent over the course of a year. In the next two grades learning in science and social studies was particularly poor, and sometimes that in mathematics slumped as well. Although some of the relative success of seventh-grade courses can be attributed to the novelty effect of television in that year, much of it is almost certainly evident only because teleclasses in grades 8 and 9 were so poor.

In the Reform's fourth year (1972), recognizing that an investment in ITV is not just an investment in electronic hardware, El Salvador's leaders again concentrated on revising the existing ITV programs and improving the teaching capabilities of the production staff. Production teams were more carefully recruited and trained, and salaries were raised so that they would not be tempted to abandon the ITV system for jobs with commercial stations. Perhaps most important, the pressure to turn out more and more programs was relaxed, and production teams were finally given sufficient time to improve the quality of their lessons.

Finally, we found no evidence that learning disparities related to age and sex within classrooms had been or could be reduced by the Reform and ITV. Younger children continued to do better than older children, and boys continued to outperform girls in both ITV and non-ITV classrooms. And the background-related disparities in intellectual skills that students exhibited at the beginning of seventh grade remained much the same throughout the Third Cycle. At the same time, there are indications that ITV and other elements of the Reform may at least have closed some of the gap related to urbanization. In general, rural classrooms still had poorer facilities than urban ones, and their teachers had less training and experience. Television was probably the only resource that was apportioned equally between rural and urban classrooms under the Reform. This trend offers some hope that where unequal learning performance is mostly the result of an unequal provision of resources, in the long run ITV may help to equalize that performance.

CHAPTER FOUR

Student Attitudes Toward School and Television

Researchers and school administrators frequently expect educational innovations like instructional television to have a positive impact not only on learning itself, but also on students' overall motivation and attitude toward school. The improvement in learning under El Salvador's Educational Reform was examined from various perspectives in Chapter 3. This chapter will analyze student attitudes toward ITV, toward particular teleseries, and toward individual subjects.

ATTITUDES TOWARD ITV

During the four years of field research, we devised a wide variety of questions to measure general student attitudes (a sample student survey is included in Appendix C). As classroom conditions changed from year to year of the Reform, so did the attitudes that required measurement. Our interim analyses of specific attitude questions also suggested a need for both substantive and stylistic revisions. As a result, no question was repeated on every survey in every year in exactly the same way. There were, however, four questions measuring students' reactions to ITV in the classroom that were phrased identically in 1971 and 1972. Cohorts A and B responded to these questions on four occasions, and Cohort C on two occasions.

Each question was a value statement about ITV, as follows:

1. "You learn more during class hours with television than during class hours without television" (reliability estimate, .521).

2. "Classes are more difficult with television" (reliability, .515).

3. "One can see the teleclasses clearly" (reliability, .428).

4. "Classroom teachers seem to prefer teaching with ITV" (reliability, .531).[1]

Three of these statements were phrased positively (i.e. in favor of ITV), and one (No. 2) was phrased negatively. For each statement, students were asked to choose the response closest to their own opinions in a list of five: "agree completely," "agree," "not sure," "disagree," and "disagree completely."

Only the responses of students in ITV classes are reported here. During the first two years of research we tried to measure the attitudes of non-ITV students as well, but this strategy was abandoned when many non-ITV students failed to express an opinion on the grounds that they had no previous experience with or knowledge of ITV. Including the responses of the non-ITV students who did answer would have biased the comparisons, since one could not prove that they were representative of the entire non-ITV sample.

Figure 4.1 presents the percentages of students in each cohort who agreed with the statements favorable to ITV or disagreed with the statement unfavorable to ITV at the beginning and end of each Third Cycle grade. (These figures should be interpreted with care, since they are fairly gross measures with neither high reliability nor exactness.) Overall, the responses showed a clear picture of high initial enthusiasm for ITV, which declined as students moved through the Third Cycle but which still remained favorable at the end of grade 9. They also indicate that each cohort was, on the average, less favorable than its predecessor.

Although 82 percent of Cohort B students at the beginning of seventh grade agreed that they would learn more from ITV classes than from non-ITV classes, this did not mean that all of them had considered the issue carefully. They had little experience with survey questionnaires, were unaccustomed to being asked their opinions, and on some questions probably had no fixed opinions. Some students were conservative in their responses and always chose the neutral alternatives; other declared themselves in complete agreement or disagreement with every statement. In addition, the questionnaires were

---

[1] Estimates are the test-retest reliability of Cohort B data for October 1970.

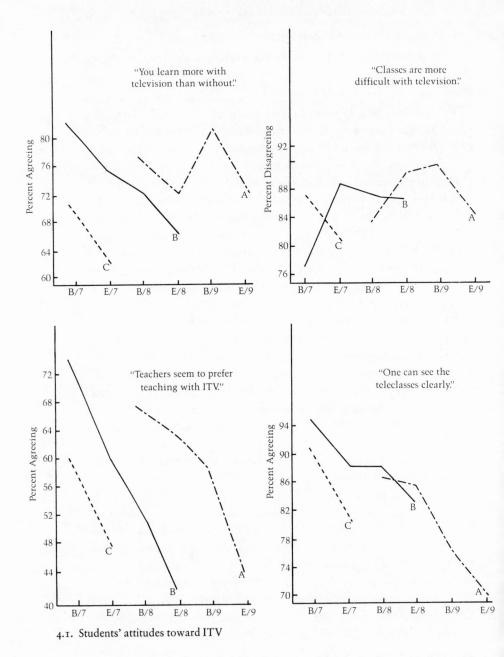

4.1. Students' attitudes toward ITV

administered by the ITV evaluation staff, often with classroom teachers looking over their shoulders. Students may have felt they were expected to express pro-ITV responses or conform to the known views of their teachers. It may be assumed, however, that all these potential sources of error and bias were uniform across measurement dates and across cohorts, making it possible to compare the attitudes of the three cohorts, as well as the attitudes of each cohort at different times, with some confidence.

If any question could be considered the basic measure of student attitudes toward ITV, it was the one comparing learning with and without television. This was posed first to Cohort A students at the beginning of eighth grade, and their responses were cyclical from that point forward; that is, at the beginning of each year expectations were high, but by the end of the year they had declined. The students of Cohort A were the pioneers of the Educational Reform, and they may have felt a special excitement and motivation as they returned to school each year. But the reality apparently did not reward their optimism; in the eighth grade they were treated to poorly made teleseries; and in the ninth grade a teachers' strike deprived them of ITV broadcasts for the last four months of the school year.

During their first two years in ITV classrooms, the favorable attitude of Cohort B students toward television declined almost 17 percent; and at parallel measurement occasions (beginning and end of eighth grade) they averaged 6 percent less acceptance of ITV than their peers in Cohort A. Similarly, Cohort C started with nearly 12 percent less acceptance than Cohort B and declined even more rapidly. By the end of grade 7, Cohort C students were more skeptical that they could "learn more from ITV" than Cohort B students had been at the end of grade 8 or Cohort A students had been after grade 9.

Certainly, these were pessimistic trends; but perhaps they should have been expected. The students entering seventh grade each year had no experience with ITV, and their television diet up to that time had consisted solely of imported cartoons, adventure series, and soap operas. The initial ITV series, produced on low budgets in a crowded studio by inexperienced teams, could hardly live up to expectations based on the far more polished commercial programs. Also, it may be that the successively lower levels of optimism expressed by each cohort at the beginning of seventh grade reflected some passing down of experience, in that students may have been warned by their older brothers and sisters that television in the classroom was really more classroom than television. It is noteworthy, however, that the majority of students in each cohort continued to feel they learned more with television. Even in Cohort C, the least favorable group at the end of seventh grade, 63 percent of the students believed that they learned more in ITV classes than in non-ITV classes, and only 10 percent felt that learning was not enhanced with ITV.

Responses to another statement, "One can see television classes clearly," followed a similar pattern. In all three cohorts agreement remained fairly high but declined over time. On the surface this statement appeared to deal only with the physical aspects of reception, but it is likely that the gradual decline in agreement reflected more than just technical difficulties or problems such as the students' eyesight. Overcrowded, noisy classrooms and a growing disenchantment with ITV may have convinced students that they could not see the lessons clearly.

Student agreement with the statement "classroom teachers seem to prefer teaching with television" declined sharply in 1971. This trend was undoubtedly related to the teachers' strike that year. Among the grievances raised by the strikers was the Ministry's decision to invest in ITV rather than higher teachers' salaries or additional classroom teaching materials. In all likelihood the students had simply not thought much about whether or not their teachers liked working with television until the issue surfaced so dramatically during the strike. Important as the strike was, however, teachers' opinions of ITV may have begun to decline much earlier, if student perceptions were correct (see Chapter 6). In any case, the teachers' resentment of Ministry policies was communicated to their students. The use of ITV in El Salvador had been predicated on the notion that classroom teachers would work in partnership with television; and when cooperation between the two was replaced by hostility and suspicion, students' attitudes and learning declined.

Attitudes Toward Individual Teleseries

To complement our investigation of students' general attitudes toward ITV, we measured attitudes toward particular teleseries. Students were asked to recommend one of three future policies for each subject that was being taught by television: (1) end the use of television in that subject; (2) continue the amount of televised instruction at its present level of 2-3 hours per week in each subject; (3) expand televised instruction to cover all class hours (4-5 hours per week in each subject). We were curious to learn how many students would prefer not to receive televised lessons. It was one thing to grumble about a specific teleseries or to express general dissatisfaction with ITV, but a different thing to propose doing without TV entirely.

As Figure 4.2 makes clear, very few students were willing to give up television completely. No more than 10 percent ever rejected ITV for science and social studies; and for English and Spanish the maximum rejections were 17 percent and 15 percent, respectively. Only in mathematics was there a substantial percentage of students (35 percent) who wished to see ITV eliminated. At the beginning of ninth grade only 5 percent of the Cohort A students wanted math without ITV, but by the end of that year the number had grown to 20 percent. Cohort B's rejection rate increased from 7 percent to 33 percent between the beginning of seventh and the end of eighth grade. Cohort C students, the most negative of the three groups, went from 6 percent to 36 percent over a comparable period.

There was no conclusive evidence on how students' attitudes toward any particular teleseries were related to their achievement in that subject. Despite its relatively low popularity, mathematics was the only subject in which the ITV subsamples consistently outachieved the non-ITV subsamples in eighth and ninth grades. In contrast, science, the most popular of all the teleseries, had the least favorable learning rate in the same grades, and non-ITV students generally outgained ITV students.

In fairness to the Salvadorean production teams, the declining popularity of the mathematics teleseries was not entirely due to the

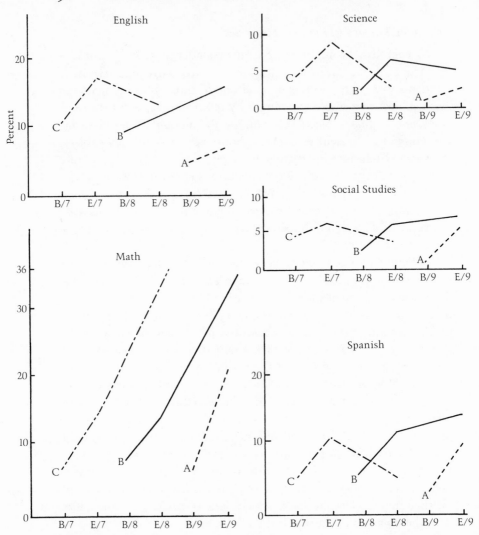

4.2. Students' attitudes toward individual teleseries

quality of the televised lessons. Students were frustrated by the subject's special vocabulary, its abstract concepts and rules, and its cumulative content structure. They had to master the early lessons or risk being confused on later ones; and this effort was probably more than that demanded in science or social studies, where students could follow a particular telelesson without having understood the previous ones and where they did not have to deal constantly with abstraction. As we shall see, the students' dislike of mathematics was not simply an unfavorable reaction to the teleseries.

Two conclusions may be drawn from the students' attitudes toward the individual teleseries. First, the introduction of television to a classroom did not automatically counteract a long history of discomfort with certain subjects, principally mathematics. Salvadorean primary teachers were poorly equipped to teach the required curricula in math, which were in any case cumbersome and difficult. As a result, many students arrived in seventh grade with inadequate preparation and a belief that mathematics was beyond their comprehension. The low scores on the initial math tests testify to the inadequacy of the students' primary training; and, although there was some learning (particularly among ITV classes) during each school year, the math telelessons did not reduce the students' basic dislike for the subject. ITV students' attitudes toward math were no more favorable than those of non-ITV students. This was probably not the fault of the math series' producers, but rather an indication that the task of the math teleseries was more difficult than that of other lessons.

The second major conclusion that may be drawn from the students' attitudes toward their courses is that liking a particular subject does not always lead to superior learning. The fact that students liked the science teleseries, for example, did not seem to enhance achievement in that subject. Although liking a subject may be a valuable precondition for strong achievement, it is clearly not sufficient in itself. In other words, keeping students happy in the classroom is not enough.

Attitudes Toward Individual Subjects

ITV and non-ITV students were also asked periodically to name their favorite and least favorite subjects among math, science, social studies, English, and Spanish. Responses were quite unstable over time. Cohort B showed the following division of preference and dislike (averaged over four measurements taken at the beginning and end of grades 7 and 8):

Favorite (N = 706)		Least favorite (N = 679)	
Mathematics	18.7%	Mathematics	32.6%
Science	26.4	Science	9.0
Social studies	23.6	Social studies	14.5
English	25.9	English	19.4
Spanish	5.3	Spanish	24.5

Students were not consistent, and relatively few chose any one subject as their most or least favored at all four measurement points.

The subject preferences for ITV and non-ITV students are compared in Table 4.1. To derive an index for each subject, we subtracted the average percentage of students expressing a negative attitude toward a particular subject on each of the four surveys from the average percentage expressing a positive attitude.

As the table reveals, attitudes toward science and social studies were positive and consistent among both ITV and non-ITV students. Attitudes toward Spanish were consistently negative. Although mathematics was the subject most disliked by both groups, ITV students were particularly negative—even though they outperformed their non-ITV peers in math. English was the one subject toward which the ITV and non-ITV subsamples held quite different attitudes: ITV students chose English as their second favorite subject, whereas non-ITV students ranked it next to last. The English programs were generally regarded as the most innovative of all the teleseries. In contrast, the teachers in non-ITV classes lacked a detailed knowledge of the language, and without television they were forced to rely on

TABLE 4.1

*Students' Attitudes Toward Individual Subjects,
With and Without ITV*

Subject	Percent naming as favorite		Percent naming as least favorite		Index of average attitude[a]	
	ITV (N = 492)	Non–ITV (N = 224)	ITV (N = 462)	Non–ITV (N = 217)	ITV (N = 462)	Non–ITV (N = 217)
Mathematics	16.1%	24.3%	34.9%	27.6%	−19.2	− 4.2
Science	27.3	24.3	9.7	7.6	+18.1	+17.4
Social studies	23.0	24.9	13.8	16.0	+ 9.4	+ 9.3
English	29.2	18.9	15.7	27.4	+13.3	− 8.8
Spanish	4.3	7.6	25.9	21.4	−21.7	−13.6

NOTE: Cohort B students only. Percentages are averages of four surveys: beginning and end of grade 7, and beginning and end of grade 8.

[a] Index for each group was calculated by subtracting the average percent naming a subject as least favorite from the average percent naming it as favorite.

rote teaching, stressing vocabulary and the repetitive practice of grammar. No comparative study was made of actual English achievement in ITV and non-ITV classrooms, but it was apparent that television had at least been successful in raising student interest in that subject.

THE INFLUENCE OF BACKGROUND VARIABLES
ON STUDENT ATTITUDES

Urbanization and general ability were related in a consistent way to the students' attitudes toward television. Rural children were more likely than urban children to say that they learned more with ITV than without ITV, that they could see the television clearly, and that their teachers preferred to teach with television. They were less inclined to believe that television classes were more difficult than classes without television. High scorers on the general ability test also tended to reject the notion that ITV classes were more difficult than non-ITV classes, although the high correlation at the beginning of seventh grade ($r = -.30$) had diminished by the end of eighth grade ($r = -.08$).[2]

In general, the background variables were better predictors of student attitudes toward specific teleseries than they were of general attitudes toward ITV. Older children, poorer children, rural children, and children whose parents had little schooling tended to be more favorable toward the teleseries than were their more advantaged peers. Similarly, children with low general ability scores were more favorable toward the ITV series. The sole exception to these patterns was the science teleseries, which was equally popular with children of all socioeconomic classes and abilities.

Attitudes toward individual subjects, irrespective of television, were also influenced by the background variables. Science was particularly well liked by wealthy, urban, young, and male students,

[2] We did not devise sophisticated models to explain the origins of student attitudes. Because the attitude measures were not reliable enough to bear the weight of such models, only bivariate analyses comparing background variables with attitudes were conducted. Complete correlation matrices of all the control variables (sex, father's education, wealth, age, urbanization and general ability) with the attitude measures described in the previous sections are presented in Appendix D.

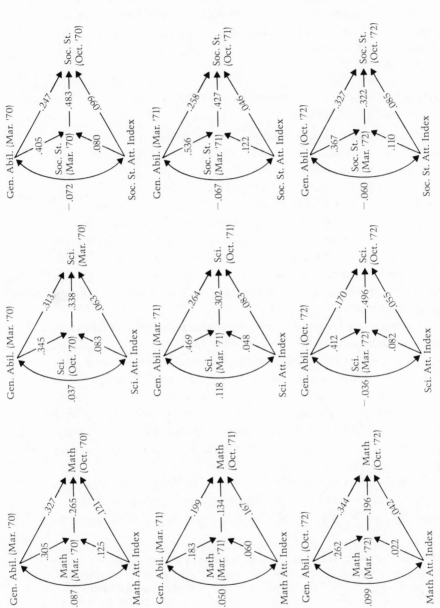

4.3. Student attitude models for Cohort B. The correlation of attitudes and March test scores with end-of-year test scores (October)

whereas Spanish was disliked by these same groups. Boys generally preferred social studies and math, and girls particularly liked English.

ATTITUDES AND LEARNING

Implicit in our decision to study student attitudes was the belief that these attitudes are closely related to academic achievement. Other things being equal, a well-motivated student should learn more than a poorly motivated one. Moreover, a student with a strong interest in a subject is more likely to continue to study it in later years and to choose a career that will demand knowledge of it. In El Salvador, students' attitudes toward individual subjects were positively related to achievement in those subjects; however, attitudes toward specific teleseries were unrelated to achievement.

Using Cohort B data, path analyses were undertaken to gauge the influence of student attitudes on achievement, over and above the influence of general ability and original competence in a subject.[3] The results are diagramed in Figure 4.3. Of prime interest are the arrows linking the students' attitudes toward specific subjects with their end-of-year test scores. Since the influence of beginning-of-year scores was eliminated, the coefficients linking attitudes and end-of-year scores are in effect estimates of the influence of attitude on achievement gains during the year. Although they were not always statistically significant, the coefficients were positive for all subjects in every grade.[4] No evidence was found linking students' attitudes toward specific ITV teleseries and learning in those subjects.

[3] The path coefficients for these particular models were identical to the regression coefficients estimated for the separate equations predicting beginning score from general ability and subject attitude and end score from beginning score, general ability, and subject attitude.

[4] There are certain methodological limitations in this type of analysis. Any variable not included in the model is assumed to be unrelated to more than one variable included in it. It is assumed that no variable (other than general ability or beginning-of-year achievement scores) affects both subject attitude and end-of-year score. Also, it is assumed that the arrows represent the true causal order of the variables—that attitude predicts achievement, and not vice versa. Since the attitude means were a composite of attitudes over four measurement waves (beginning and end of grades 7 and 8), one may wonder whether good early achievement in a subject could have positively affected observed enthusiasm for the subject rather than the reverse. However, the fact that the attitude measures were still related to grade 9 achievement, which took place after the measurement of the attitudes, supports the inference that attitudes influenced achievement.

The large coefficients relating general ability scores to end-of-year achievement scores left little doubt that bright children out-performed their less able classmates. However, the bright group's learning edge was probably overestimated in these coefficients because of statistical artifacts related to the superior reliability of the general ability test in contrast to the learning tests.[5]

SUMMARY AND IMPLICATIONS

The collection of actual learning data, as we have seen, was supplemented by periodic surveys of students' attitudes toward ITV in general, toward particular teleseries, and toward particular classroom subjects. Only students in ITV classes responded to questions in the first two categories, whereas all students answered questions in the third category. Although a majority of students remained favorable toward ITV in every survey, high initial enthusiasm for the new system declined as students progressed through the Third Cycle. When asked if they would prefer to do without one or more of the teleseries, few students said yes. However, at the last measurement one-third of the eighth- and ninth-graders in ITV classrooms said they would like to eliminate the math teleseries.

Attitudes toward science and social studies were positive among both ITV and non-ITV students; Spanish and math were disliked by both subsamples, although math was particularly unpopular among ITV students. English was very well liked by ITV students and little liked by their counterparts in non-ITV classes. Disadvantaged children and children with low general ability were more favorably disposed toward the teleseries than their more advantaged peers. Only science was equally well liked by all strata of students.

Sex influenced the choice of favorite subject, with boys leaning toward science, social studies and math, and girls toward English and Spanish. And choice of math, science, or social studies as a student's favorite subject positively influenced his gain on achievement tests in the subject.

The relationship of attitudes to learning is a complex one. Most educators assume that without a strong desire to learn, students will

[5] Cf. D. A. Wiley and R. Hornik, "Measurement error and the analysis of panel data." *Mehr Licht: Studies of Educative Processes*, Rept. 5, Aug. 1973.

become bored and absorb little in the classroom. In El Salvador, as in other developing countries, the strongest motivation to stay in school may well be extrinsic: the belief that a diploma is the best guarantee of eventually finding a good job. Yet long-range employment goals probably do not provide sufficient motivation for students, for school is a day-to-day affair. If what a student is studying is of little or no intrinsic interest, his or her ability to take advantage of schooling is likely to diminish over time.

One of the attractive aspects of television is its potential as a motivating device, and Salvadorean students were excited by the introduction of the medium to their classrooms. It was quite possible that the higher achievement in seventh-grade television classes was related to this enthusiasm. However, the motivating effect was not long-lasting; and within each of the cohorts enthusiasm waned when ITV ceased to be something new. But the positive regard of ITV students for English, in contrast to a general dislike for the subject among non-ITV students, indicated that this waning was not inevitable. The continuing success of the English teleseries confirms what many advocates of instructional television have suggested: television can be particularly effective in teaching subjects for which a classroom teacher is ill prepared. Music and foreign languages, for example, are often beyond the scope of the average classroom teacher, and most developing countries cannot afford to hire specialists to teach them. Here ITV can fulfill a vital role long after teachers have stopped relying on television in other subjects.

The enthusiasm of disadvantaged and less able students for television teleseries may be attributed to several possible causes. ITV was particularly popular among poor students, who were concentrated in rural communities where schools often had the barest resources and the least prepared and experienced teaching staffs. As a result, television loomed larger for them than it did for their counterparts in the richer urban schools. This finding was an encouraging one. As enrollment at all levels increases in El Salvador, ITV's potential as a motivator is likely to remain quite large among the poor, rural children who will make up the bulk of the classroom audience.

CHAPTER FIVE

Student Aspirations

An underlying premise of El Salvador's Educational Reform was that the nation's development required not only citizens who were more educated, but also people trained in a broad range of the middle-level administrative and technical skills needed in new industries. Accordingly, free basic education was extended from six to nine years; and secondary education beyond the ninth grade was diversified and acquired a greater emphasis on technical training programs.

In the traditional system, secondary schooling had been almost exclusively the preserve of upper-class students bound for the university. However, since the Reform brought a threefold expansion in Third Cycle enrollment, most secondary students could no longer realistically aspire to a higher education. Salvadorean planners were simply not willing to allocate additional resources to expand the university system. Although new technical training programs were being set up at the advanced secondary level (*bachillerato*), even these would not be able to absorb the thousands of new ninth-grade graduates. Noting these changes, the Ministry of Education, as part of its second five-year plan, set a 60-percent limit on the number of secondary students who would be allowed to continue their education beyond ninth grade.[1] Implicit in the plans for expansion and diversification was the expectation that students would

[1] ODEPOR, *Plan Quinquenal del ramo educación* (San Salvador, 1973), p. 21.

soon have to abandon the traditional view of secondary school as a stepping-stone to the university.

During the first year of our evaluation study (1969), we discovered that secondary students held startlingly high educational and occupational aspirations. In 1969, only 6 percent of the seventh-graders surveyed (Cohort A) planned to leave school after the ninth grade; but 54 percent expected to obtain an advanced secondary degree, and 40 percent had set their sights on the university. Because these students had enrolled in grade 7 before the great expansion, many could reasonably expect to fulfill their aspirations. However, students who entered in later years were sure to be disappointed if they maintained similar hopes.

We wished to determine whether the Ministry's new conception of the ninth grade as the final year of education for most students would be accepted by students and reflected in a lowering of their aspirations. The question was examined in four ways. First, the students' educational and occupational aspirations were measured as they entered seventh grade and were monitored continuously thereafter. Second, the influence of various background variables on these aspirations was analyzed. Third, a study of Salvadorean parents was undertaken to determine what influence they had on student aspirations and to see how this influence related to the parents' own educational and career backgrounds. Finally, in an attempt to go beyond the hypothetical aspirations that were expressed by students on survey questionnaires, the first ninth-grade graduates under the Reform were interviewed midway through the year following their graduation to determine whether their hopes had been realized.

EDUCATIONAL ASPIRATIONS

A battery of survey questions administered over six measurement waves and four years was used to gather data on students' educational aspirations (see the sample student survey in Appendix C). The repetition of identical questions over time permitted changes in aspirations to be charted as students passed through the three years of the Third Cycle. Although it was not possible to determine whether the aspirations that students expressed represented realistic

TABLE 5.1
Educational Aspirations of Three Student Cohorts
on All Measurement Waves

Cohort and aspiration	Grade 7		Grade 8		Grade 9	
	Begin	End	Begin	End	Begin	End
Cohort A (N = 902)						
Finish Third Cycle	10.7%	4.1%	5.2%	4.9%	2.2%	2.2%
Finish secondary	53.6	44.9	55.3	50.7	46.6	42.6
Finish university	35.7	51.0	39.4	44.3	51.3	55.1
Cohort B (N = 707)						
Finish Third Cycle	9.2	6.3	2.8	3.7	—	2.4
Finish secondary	52.6	47.9	43.3	38.2	—	43.9
Finish university	38.1	45.8	53.0	58.1	—	53.6
Cohort C (N = 600)						
Finish Third Cycle	9.6	6.9	—	6.6	—	—
Finish secondary	45.7	46.3	—	45.3	—	—
Finish university	44.6	46.9	—	48.2	—	—

expectations or mere fantasies, the responses at least suggested how far they would like to go in school under ideal circumstances (see Table 5.1).

The aspirations of Cohort A students rose dramatically during the Third Cycle. The proportion of students who were content to continue their schooling only through grade 9 diminished by about 9 percent over three years, and those wishing to stop after advanced secondary studies declined by about 11 percent; by contrast the proportion aiming at university studies increased by about 20 percent, and by the beginning of grade 9 this group included the majority of students in Cohort A. Cohort B students followed a similar pattern, and finished grade 9 with students divided among the three aspiration levels almost identically with Cohort A.

Although Cohort C students came from relatively poorer homes than did Cohort A or B students, and usually from families where the parents had less formal education, their educational aspirations were quite similar to those of the other cohorts. However, the changes in aspirations were less dramatic in this group, at least up to the end of eighth grade. Cohort C had higher educational aspirations at the beginning of seventh grade and maintained these through eighth grade, whereas Cohorts A and B started lower but rose faster over the same period.

OCCUPATIONAL ASPIRATIONS

Over four years students were also periodically asked to specify what careers they wished to enter after they finished school (see Table 5.2). Occupational choices were divided into three levels, according to how much schooling would be required to qualify for different jobs. The first level required little or no education; the second included the skilled trades that customarily demanded some secondary schooling beyond the Third Cycle; and the third required some postsecondary or professional training.

The students' occupational aspirations were in general quite comparable to their educational aspirations. Where there was inconsistency, the data indicated that the students simply desired more education than was customarily required to qualify for a given job. Students also elevated their job aspirations during the Third Cycle. However, when the survey data were compared, it was evident that lower occupational aspirations had been expressed by each succeeding cohort. There was no corresponding decline in the pattern of educational aspirations, which suggests that the students were probably being quite realistic. In El Salvador's tight job market the educational requirements for all jobs are continually rising, and the students most likely realized that it would be wise to get as much

TABLE 5.2
Occupational Aspirations of Three Student Cohorts
on All Measurement Waves

Cohort and aspiration	Grade 7		Grade 8		Grade 9	
	Begin	End	Begin	End	Begin	End
Cohort A (N = 902)						
Level 1	6.8%	2.6%	2.3%	2.2%	2.3%	1.8%
Level 2	59.4	55.1	60.1	56.9	52.7	54.0
Level 3	33.8	42.3	37.6	40.9	45.0	44.2
Cohort B (N = 707)						
Level 1	2.5	2.6	1.7	2.0	—	5.9
Level 2	62.5	56.9	53.3	50.9	—	54.2
Level 3	35.0	40.5	45.0	47.1	—	39.9
Cohort C (N = 600)						
Level 1	3.4	2.6	—	4.5	—	—
Level 2	67.1	63.7	—	57.9	—	—
Level 3	29.5	33.7	—	37.6	—	—

schooling as possible before going to work, regardless of the level of job they wanted.

SEX DIFFERENCES IN STUDENT ASPIRATIONS

Important differences appeared in the relative aspiration levels of boys and girls (see Appendix Tables D.15 and D.16). From 7 to 17 percent more boys than girls wanted a university education the last time aspirations were measured in each cohort, and there were even sharper differences in career preferences. Fewer girls than boys planned on professional careers, but the gap narrowed somewhat over the three years of the Third Cycle. By the end of ninth grade 51 percent of Cohort A boys chose professional careers, as opposed to 35 percent of Cohort A girls. In Cohort B, the percentages were 45 and 33, respectively; and in Cohort C (end of grade 8), 44 and 27.

A few occupations were favored by both boys and girls, notably doctor, teacher, and accountant. Others were selected exclusively by one group: nurse or secretary by girls; engineer, mechanic, industrial tchnician, lawyer, or agronomist by boys. The career preferences of girls were relatively few, with nursing the overwhelming first choice in all three cohorts. Boys expressed a much greater variety of aspirations.

The attraction of medicine for both boys and girls is easily understood, since it is one of the most respected and lucrative professions in El Salvador. It was a particularly strong choice among students from urban areas and from the higher socioeconomic groups. Accounting was a strong choice among rural and lower-class students. This is one of the few white-collar jobs in El Salvador that does not require an advanced-secondary or university degree. Actually, the career of *contador* (accountant) in El Salvador implies a greater range of clerical positions than might customarily be associated with the term, and many students who receive the contador degree do not find work as accountants, eventually accepting other office jobs. But because the degree indicates at least some advanced (i.e. postsecondary) education, it is viewed as a step toward higher-status positions. Consequently, it has a strong appeal, particularly to the poorer rural families.

The large differences in the aspirations of boys and girls were not particularly surprising. Like the parallel sex differences related to learning that we discussed in Chapter 3, the results here are consistent with studies conducted in other parts of the world. Sex differences in the aspiration levels of secondary-school students reflect deeply rooted cultural attitudes and values, which affect not only how boys and girls form career goals and appraise different job opportunities, but also how well they achieve in school. The following sections will examine these factors in more detail and discuss how much they appear to have influenced aspirations in El Salvador.

THE ORIGIN OF STUDENT ASPIRATIONS

Within the pattern of high educational and occupational aspirations, there was considerable variation among Salvadorean students. In order to identify the sources of this variation, and to determine which students would be likely to seek university degrees and which would be satisfied with alternative academic programs, we examined the relationship between aspirations and various background variables. As in Chapter 3, six variables were defined: sex, age, father's education, wealth, urbanization, and general ability. A three-point aspiration index was created out of the students' responses to various survey questions: 2 was assigned to students who aspired to both a university education and a professional career; 1 was assigned to students who aspired either to the university or to an occupation requiring advanced training, but not to both; and 0 was assigned to students who had lower aspirations in both categories.

Within each cohort, and across all measurement waves, there was a consistent relationship between the aspiration index and the control variables. Boys held higher aspirations than girls. Children of well-educated parents, children from wealthier homes, and children who entered the Third Cycle at a lower age all expressed higher aspirations than their companions. The correlations are presented in Table 5.3. General ability test scores were a somewhat different case: they were positively related to aspiration levels, but the relationship was little higher than might have been predicted from the strong relation between the other background variables and general ability (see Chapter 3).

TABLE 5.3

*Correlations Between Student Aspiration Indexes and
Background Variables in Three Student Cohorts*

	Aspiration index					
	Cohort A (N = 902)		Cohort B (N = 707)		Cohort C (N = 600)	
Variable	Beg. gr. 7	End gr. 9	Beg. gr. 7	End gr. 9	Beg. gr. 7	End gr. 8
Sex[a]	.21	.20	.11	.11	.15	.18
Age	−.18	−.15	−.21	−.25	−.17	−.23
Father's education	.20	.21	.26	.25	.22	.34
Wealth	.24	.22	.23	.28	.33	.35
Urbanization[b]	.13	.21	.07	.20	.24	.31
General ability	.17	.18	.19	.27	.22	.27

[a] Female = 0, male = 1.
[b] Rural = 1, urban = 5.

Because the background variables themselves were all significantly related to general ability—and, with the possible exception of age, could be viewed as causally precedent to it—a useful procedure for examining the effect of general ability on aspirations was to estimate the amount of variance in aspiration accounted for by general ability over and above the variance accounted for by the five other variables. We chose to compare our three sample groups as they entered seventh grade; that is, at the beginning of the Third Cycle:

	Cohort A (N = 703)	Cohort B (N = 591)	Cohort C (N = 462)
Variance accounted for by five control variables: sex, age, father's education, wealth, and urbanization	.129	.117	.154
Variance accounted for by these control variables plus general ability score	.135	.122	.161

General ability level, then, predicted no more than 1 percent of the additional variance in aspiration in any of the three cohorts entering grade 7. Although each of the other five control variables was significantly related to aspiration, altogether they did not account for more than 16 percent of the variance in aspiration within any cohort. In other words, 84 percent of the variance in student aspiration at the outset of the Third Cycle was attributable to other influences.[2] When this analysis was extended to aspiration levels at the end of grade 9 (end of grade 8 for Cohort C), a sizeable increment in the predictive power of the five background variables was observed only in Cohort C, where the explained variance was .230. (Cohort A was .128, and Cohort B .147.) There was clearly a great deal more to the formation of aspiration than the interplay of student background characteristics.

The background factors did prove useful in helping to predict what the aspirations of future Salvadorean students are likely to be. Assuming that the processes underlying the formation of aspirations will remain the same, it is possible to estimate what effects changes in the social makeup of future student cohorts will have on aspiration levels.[3] As the number of students enrolled at each academic level increased under the Reform, the background characteristics of the average student changed quite radically; in particular, more children from El Salvador's lower classes gained access to school for the first time. This trend seems likely to continue. Whether a continuing decline in average social background will make very much difference in students' expectations for their futures is an open question. Assuming a maximum shift in social background, the best

[2] Estimates of explained variance implicitly assume that all variables were measured in perfectly reliable fashion. This assumption was untenable here, and the reliability of the aspiration index was probably between .55 and .65. Since unreliability implies an underestimate of explained variance, the reported estimates could have been underestimated by 50-100 percent. Even assuming such an error, however, approximately 70 percent of the variance would still be unexplained.

[3] These assumptions may be incorrect. If more and more Salvadorean students are forced to leave school at the end of the ninth grade, it may be that students entering seventh grade will notice the trend and lower their aspirations accordingly. An additional assumption of such forecasting is that the processes involved are essentially linear: that the change in the dependent variable resulting from a given increment in the independent variable will be the same no matter where in the range of the independent variable that increment occurs. For example, using a five-point urbanization scale, it is assumed that a change from 0 to 1 on that scale will have the same effect on aspirations as a change from 4 to 5. This is a general assumption in all correlation analyses; but it is particularly critical when one wishes to make predictions about populations whose characteristics may be quite different than the population for which the parameters were estimated originally.

estimate would be that approximately 35 percent of all students will aspire to university careers, and almost all the rest to a high-school education. This contrasts with 58 percent aspiring to the university and the rest to high school in Cohort B of our sample.

Thus, no matter what their background, students will continue to aspire to careers that traditionally have offered prestige and the best chance to earn a good salary. This orientation bodes well for El Salvador's educational and industrial planners—provided they can offer enough of the future graduates job opportunities in the modern sector of the economy. Lacking these opportunities, the majority of students who terminate their educations short of the university will continue to aspire to the more traditional white-collar positions, which are already overcrowded.

PARENTAL ATTITUDES AND STUDENT ASPIRATIONS

In 1970, the third year of the Reform, a special study was undertaken to explore parental attitudes and their relation to student aspirations. The interview sample included 247 parents of eighth-grade boys, and was divided into subgroups according to urban or rural residence, son's enrollment in an ITV or non-ITV class, and son's aspiration level. Primarily, we wished to learn what importance Salvadoreans placed on education in their own lives and in the lives of their children. From the student survey data, we had learned that most parents of Third Cycle students had not themselves completed primary school. Yet these same parents had managed to provide for the education of their sons, who, by virtue of having reached the Third Cycle, were much more likely to gain access to the privileged strata of their society.

More than 90 percent of the parents we interviewed deemed their own level of schooling insufficient and said they wished they could have gone further. How much more schooling they desired and their reasons for wanting it varied according to how far they had actually gone in school and according to their social backgrounds. A majority of parents in the most rural areas, and a majority of mothers at all urbanization levels, simply wished that they had finished primary school. The motives of these respondents were also the most explicit: with more education, they felt, they would have been able to qualify for steady and better-paying jobs. Parents at the higher urbanization levels considered a commercial "short course" (*carrera corta*) the suitable amount of additional schooling; this training was viewed as an entry to a variety of white-collar positions. The relatively few parents (44) who had studied beyond the ninth grade envisioned a university degree as the right amount of additional education. These parents tended to justify their desires in more abstract terms, and placed more importance on the intangible satisfactions of being an "educated person."

Images of enslavement and servitude were common in the parents' assessments of their own careers. Because they lacked a primary or secondary certificate, many parents doubted that they would ever escape the threat of unemployment. Indeed, it was not the low level of their present jobs that preoccupied them, but the fear that without proper schooling all jobs would become increasingly difficult to obtain. Secure employment was also a condition that parents mentioned as affecting their intentions to help their sons stay in school. More than a third of the parents said that one major reason they wished they had more schooling was that this would have enabled them to help their children more.

Few Salvadorean parents, if any, will ever have an opportunity to return to school. Yet their desire to do so and the level of education they aspired to could be expected to play an important part in the amount of encouragement and support they gave their sons.

PARENTS' KNOWLEDGE OF SCHOOLS AND THE EDUCATIONAL REFORM

At the outset of the study, we assumed that most Salvadorean parents had only limited contact with their sons' schools. This view was based on estimates of the parents' low educational levels and on our feeling that parents might be ill at ease with school directors or teachers, whose advanced education might be intimidating. Also, a continuing scarcity of operating funds often forced many school directors to solicit local financial support on their own, which could well deter poor parents from forming close ties with a school. In spite of these obstacles, however, we hypothesized at least a limited relationship between parental contacts with the schools and the aspiration levels of both students and parents.

Surprisingly, we soon discovered that 83 percent of the respondents had visited their sons' schools at least once during 1970. The prime reason for these visits had been to pay tuition, but nearly 70 percent of the parents said they had also taken the opportunity to discuss a son's progress with one or more of his teachers. As expected, urban fathers had had the most contact with their sons' schools, and mothers from rural areas the least.

Although El Salvador's Educational Reform had been under way for over two years and had received nationwide publicity before our study, 55 percent of the parents could not remember ever having heard or read about it. Their relative awareness could not be entirely explained by controlling for a school category such as ITV or non-ITV. In fact, this particular control procedure revealed an unexpected trend: parents of boys in non-ITV classes knew more about the Reform than parents of boys in the ITV classes. This finding appeared to contradict what we had interpreted as a widespread appreciation of the Reform on the basis of parents' responses to an earlier question about school attributes. Additional analysis revealed that urbanization was the key intervening variable in knowledge of the Reform. Three-quarters of the parents from San Salvador knew of the Reform, as compared with less than half the parents in the other three urbanization categories. In the most rural areas, not one parent in five had heard of the Reform.

Among parents who were aware of the Reform, only ITV and the teacher retraining program were mentioned by more than 10 percent as specific Reform programs. ITV was referred to most often, and many parents claimed they had seen one or more telecasts at home or in their sons' schools. Subsequent questions revealed that these parents usually had highly positive attitudes toward ITV, even though most did not realize that televised instruction was an integral part of the comprehensive Reform program. We measured parental opinions about five aspects of the ITV system: student learning and motivation; the role of the classroom teacher; TV's effect on student eyesight; and future expansion of the ITV system.

Responses varied according to whether or not the parent actually had a son in an ITV class. When the son was receiving televised instruction, parental attitudes were extremely favorable, regardless of parents' sex or urbanization level. Among parents whose sons were in non-ITV classes, less positive attitudes predominated, particularly in the urban areas. This trend could be explained in part by the special status of the two schools that provided our urban non-ITV sample. Both were among the small group of institutions in El Salvador that required students to pass an entrance examination, and both have long been rated as among the best public schools in the country. It is conceivable that the introduction of television in these schools was viewed by parents as a leveling force that would deprive their sons of the rather special status conferred by the schools' superior reputation.

Although a majority of the parents of sons in rural non-ITV classes expressed moderately negative attitudes toward ITV on the question battery, 80 percent of this group later said they would favor an expansion of the system. This inconsistency may be attributed to the fact that most rural parents simply had little information about ITV; and their responses to the interview questions probably reflected intuitive judgments or prejudices based on their viewing of commercial television. For example, in response to a question about the quality of student learning with television, one rural father remarked, "Only robbery and killing are taught on television." This same man, learning more about the ITV system during the course of the interview, later changed his opinion considerably.

In sum, the interest parents took in local schools varied widely. A majority of the mothers—and virtually all the respondents in the most rural group—were unable to specify any school characteristic they either liked or wished to see changed. Knowledge of the Educational Reform was also limited, although most parents were favorably disposed toward ITV when specifically asked about it.

PARENTS' EDUCATIONAL ASPIRATIONS

Salvadorean parents proved to be in much closer contact with the schools than we had expected, and to take a greater interest in the methods and goals of the educational system. Since the Ministry of Education had had definite goals in mind when it instituted ITV and the other Reform measures, in the sense that it was aiming at an educated work force with new kinds of training and job qualification, one must naturally ask whether the aspirations of parents

TABLE 5.4
Parents' and Sons' Educational Aspirations

Sample	Finish grade 9	Finish advanced secondary course	Finish university
Parents, Sept. 1970 (N = 247)	9%	52%	39%
Sons, Mar. 1970 (N = 247)	9	39	43
Sons, Oct. 1970 (N = 231)	5	37	58

and students were consistent with the government's plans. Insofar as the parents' ideas of proper education could influence their children's performance under the Reform, these ideas could be expected to contribute to the overall success or failure of the Reform programs. An important objective of our study, then, was to learn not only how far Salvadorean parents wanted their sons to go in school, but also the reasons behind these choices and the strength of the parents' commitment to them. Accordingly, the interviews were structured both to elicit the parents' preferences and to test their consistency.

Table 5.4 shows the levels of schooling that parents desired for their sons, as well as the levels the sons themselves aspired to at the beginning and end of eighth grade. The parents' aspirations for their sons were strongly related to the demographic variables discussed earlier. Seventy-five percent of the parents living in San Salvador wanted their sons to continue through secondary school or university, whereas less than 40 percent of the parents from the most rural areas held a similar preference. Mothers in general had lower aspirations than fathers. A majority of the mothers said they wanted their sons to study no more than the commercial "short courses" available to ninth-grade graduates; only 35 percent of the fathers agreed that this schooling would be sufficient.

When the urbanization variable was controlled, sex differences were qualified somewhat (see Table 5.5). The aspirations of urban mothers fell between those of the urban and rural fathers; but rural mothers were heavily concentrated at the lower half of the scale, and less than 35 percent wanted their sons to study beyond a *carrera corta*. The high incidence of missing husbands and the poverty of many rural families in El Salvador suggests that rural mothers were

TABLE 5.5
*Educational Aspirations of Mothers and Fathers for Sons,
Controlled for Urbanization*

Sample	Finish Third Cycle	Finish short course	Finish bachillerato	Finish university
Urban fathers (N = 74)	5%	28%	15%	51%
Urban mothers (N = 67)	5	34	18	43
Rural fathers (N = 46)	11	30	24	35
Rural mothers (N = 59)	15	53	8	24

counting on their sons to become breadwinners as soon as possible.

To clarify the rationale behind the parents' aspirations, we asked them to specify what advantages there would be in advanced schooling for their sons. The number of different advantages parents could name was covariant to a significant degree with their own education and with the education they wanted for their sons. Thus 42 percent of the parents with no schooling and 57 percent of the parents at the lowest aspiration level could not give more than one reason why their sons should finish ninth grade. In contrast, over 45 percent of the well-educated parents, and the same proportion of those who wanted their sons to reach the university, were able to name three or more advantages.

Three underlying themes were apparent in the many different advantages Salvadorean parents associated with schooling for their sons. Of prime importance to over 40 percent of the sample were the kinds of jobs a young man could qualify for by staying in school beyond the ninth grade. Any sort of advanced academic training—short course, bachillerato, or university—might lead to a career that would guarantee the son, and indirectly his parents, a more secure future.

A second theme was that of self-esteem. Parents who cited this "advantage" also mentioned the need for their sons to act independently and with self-confidence in the larger society. Educated men, they felt, could not be taken advantage of in ordinary business affairs. The patriotic feeling that educated people were of greater value to the nation was also frequently mentioned in this connection.

The final theme, encompassing about a quarter of the parents' responses, was that of "helping the family." To be sure, this advantage was related to employment, but it was expressed with a direct-ness and sincerity that deserves special mention. Parents who envi-sioned such an "advantage" emphasized the important and respon-sible role that an educated son would ultimately be expected to play in his family. Generally, they were poor and from rural areas; and they seemed to regard an educated son as an "emissary" to the out-side world, who would eventually return to provide for other mem-bers of the family.

When parents were asked what occupation they would most like to see their sons enter after completing school, 33 percent favored a professional career, 47 percent a middle-level occupation, and 20 percent a low-level job. These selections were somewhat less ambi-tious than those of the boys themselves (who chose high-level jobs 50 percent of the time, and low-level jobs only 3 percent); but it was clear that the parents' hopes for their sons had not been unduly restrained by how they regarded their own life situations.

The usual variations according to sex and place of residence ap-peared in the job preferences stated by parents. Although a middle-level career was the most common choice of respondents of both sexes, whether rural or urban, there were substantial differences in the proportions choosing high- and low-level occupations. Forty per-cent of all male parents desired a professional career for their sons, as against 27 percent of the female respondents. By coincidence, ex-actly the same percentages characterized urban and rural respon-dents, respectively. As expected, rural women held the lowest aspi-rations for their sons, more than 25 percent mentioning a low-level job as their first choice.

It is also interesting to compare the five careers most frequently named by parents with those chosen by their sons earlier in the year:

Parents	Sons
Accountant (26%)	Engineer (19%)
Doctor (10%)	Accountant (13%)
Engineer (8%)	Doctor (12%)
Agronomist (8%)	Bachiller (10%)[4]
Mechanic (7%)	Agronomist (8%)

[4] In these cases the sons had no plans beyond getting a degree and qualifying for higher training.

On the surface it would appear that there was considerable agreement between parents and sons, and that the two generations overlapped in their ideas of the most desirable occupations in El Salvador. To determine whether this overlap was coincidental or the result of personal interaction, the parents were asked if they knew their sons' job preferences, and if so, to state what these were. As a measure of the consistency between generations, the actual choices of the boys were then cross-tabulated with the ones their parents attributed to them.

Sixty-eight percent of the parents said they knew what jobs their sons aspired to, and this proportion did not vary substantially when the groups were broken down by sex, urbanization, or socioeconomic status. However, when the choices the boys had made at the beginning of the year were matched against the ones their parents had indicated, it was discovered that there was agreement in only 25 percent of the cases. Most likely, the majority of parents were not really aware of their sons' choices but were reluctant to admit this. When asked to be specific, therefore, they gave what amounted to their best guesses, which may have been based largely on their own preferences for their sons.

With few exceptions, we discovered that Salvadorean parents had little regular contact with their sons' schools at least in the sense that they could actually evaluate classroom conditions; yet they placed a tremendous value on education per se. Perhaps because of their own lack of experience with education, parents did not seem to have directly influenced the educational aspirations or expectations of their sons. Rather, their influence had been indirect and tied closely to underlying variations in their own educational experiences, social class, sex, and place of residence. The ability to obtain a steady, well-paying job was the sole justification for advanced schooling in the eyes of most parents. The positions they envisioned for their sons paralleled the choices the sons themselves had made, but there was little evidence that families had discussed this topic among themselves. Nevertheless, the occupational aspirations of both generations were concentrated largely on the careers that have traditionally promised social mobility and prestige in El Salvador.

THE FOLLOW-UP STUDY OF THIRD CYCLE GRADUATES

One might reasonably view the whole question of student aspirations with some skepticism. Were the aspirations expressed on students' questionnaires true expectations, or were they just the dreams of young people who knew very well that they would probably have to settle for much less? One attempt to clarify this question was made in the questionnaires themselves (see Appendix C). Students were asked how confident they were of actually fulfilling their educational aspirations; their second-choice aspirations were solicited; and they were asked how willing they would be to leave school after the ninth grade if a good job was offered them. The responses to such questions were ambiguous, and in the end they neither confirmed nor contradicted the students' expressed intentions.

Another method used to test the validity of the student aspiration data was a follow-up study of students who had completed the Third Cycle. To this end, a sample of 400 Cohort A students was interviewed in 1972, the year after they left ninth grade. Our objectives were to discover what had become of the first group of students educated under the Reform and to determine whether or not their careers conformed to the aspirations they had expressed before graduation.

For the great majority of students in the sample, educational aspirations were indeed being fulfilled. Of the 392 graduates who were finally interviewed, 336 were continuing their education. Moreover, there was virtually no difference between graduates of ITV and non-ITV classrooms in the percentage of graduates still in school. A slightly higher proportion of girls were pursuing full-time studies; but when the "studying and working part-time" group was added to the "studying only" group, the proportions of boys and girls enrolled in some sort of academic program were about equal. About half of those continuing their education were enrolled in a bachillerato program in the same city or town where they had finished ninth grade; the rest were either commuting to other cities and towns daily (26 percent) or had moved elsewhere (24 percent). The pursuit of advanced training, then, was accelerating the migration of Third Cycle graduates to the bigger towns and cities, a trend likely to retard the development of El Salvador's rural areas and intensify the overcrowding of its urban areas.

About 50 percent of the graduates who were continuing their education were enrolled in an academic bachillerato and preparing for the university. Of the rest, 32 percent were studying commercial or business administration, 8 percent were learning industrial trades, and about 10 percent were dispersed among the various advanced programs newly established by the Reform (e.g., agriculture, fishing and navigation, hygiene and health, hotel and tourist trades, teacher training, and fine arts). The reasons these students gave for continuing varied widely: to undertake university studies; to better chances for a good job; to improve one's general knowledge; or to earn some academic degree or title.

All the graduates in the sample (including those who were "only working" or "neither working nor studying") were also asked to specify future plans. The majority planned to continue their studies either full-time or part-time, and 88 percent of these opted for one of the bachillerato programs (only 9 percent indicated an interest in lower-level study programs). Whether or not students planned to attend the university, most indicated that they did not want to lose the option of eventually doing so.

We could not determine, of course, how many Third Cycle graduates would actually finish the bachillerato and go on to the university. But there can be little doubt that the aspirations expressed by this group reflected a genuine commitment, especially considering that 25 percent of the sample had changed their residences in order to attend a bachillerato. Still, half the ninth-grade graduates still in school were enrolled in traditional academic programs leading to the university. Apparently, Salvadorean young people still hoped to reach high-level administrative and professional posts rather than enter the middle-level technical and business careers that the educational reformers had hoped to encourage. However, one must remember that educational reform alone may not be enough. The large percentage of ninth-grade graduates who were continuing their studies was also an indication of how difficult it is for young people to find work in El Salvador. Of the 56 graduates who were not studying full-time, almost half were unemployed. Social unrest and political turbulence may increase in the near future if appropriate jobs cannot be provided for the increasing numbers of graduates.

SUMMARY AND IMPLICATIONS

In reporting of survey results, one often tends to become lost among variables and statistically significant relationships, thereby losing sight of the very human motivations and hopes that first seemed worthy of study. The purpose of this chapter has been two-fold: to summarize the survey data collected on student aspirations over four years, and to illuminate in a qualitative way what Salvadorean students and their parents actually thought about the education the former were receiving and the careers they were heading toward. Unfortunately, it was not really possible to determine whether the Reform had produced great changes in student aspirations, since we had no comparable baseline data from before 1969. But the data we did gather conveyed one clear warning: the aspirations of students for both education and jobs were so high as to present a real problem to Salvadorean planners in the immediate future.

Advanced schooling was clearly regarded by students as the key to success in El Salvador. More than 90 percent of the students surveyed in each of the three cohorts wished to continue their studies beyond the ninth grade, and approximately 50 percent hoped to obtain a university degree. In the first two student cohorts, the desire for advanced studies increased over time; in the third cohort, a high level of educational aspiration was expressed at the very beginning and retained throughout. In all these groups, how far a student aspired to go in school and how confident he was of getting there varied according to his socioeconomic status, place of residence, and general ability (although general ability did not appear to exert as much influence as other factors). Boys from the higher social strata who lived in an urban area were the most desirous of pursuing a university career.

The students' occupational aspirations were still more closely tied to their origins. However, the desire for professional employment was high among all but the most rural students. The perceived status of different jobs was of great importance, and this status was apparently determined by traditional values and by the academic degrees customarily required to qualify for different positions. The consistency between students' educational and occupational aspirations indicated that they had not made random responses to our questions but had probably given some prior thought to their choices.

Given El Salvador's high unemployment and the shortage of well-paying jobs at the middle levels, it is understandable that so many students aspired to university careers. They apparently recognized that the best jobs would continue to be awarded to university graduates, and that a good job would offer the best guarantee of social prestige and mobility in the years ahead. To this extent, their aspirations must be considered realistic. These same aspirations must be considered unrealistic, however, in terms of the students' actual chances for fulfilling them. In fact, the probability of a given student's continuing through the university will actually be reduced if the enrollment projections of the Reform are eventually realized.

Salvadorean parents expressed generally lower educational and occupational aspirations for their sons than the sons had for themselves. However, there was considerable variation among the parents according to sex, urbanization, and socioeconomic status. Urban fathers who had some schooling beyond the primary level held the highest aspirations for their sons; rural mothers, who rarely had completed more than one or two years of school, expressed the lowest aspirations. All parents placed great importance on education for their children, but their ability to provide guidance was limited by their own lack of education and by their lack of knowledge of El Salvador's school system and the Educational Reform. Little evidence was found to suggest that they had consciously attempted to influence their sons' aspirations. In fact, most parents claimed they would support whatever their sons decided to do, although their magnanimity was often tempered by an admission that it would be difficult for them to pay all the expenses of an advanced academic program.

We found that students tended to justify their high aspirations in idealistic and often altruistic terms. The parents were more practical: Advanced schooling was necessary, most believed, only because it would enable their children to obtain good jobs. Moreover, a son with greater earning potential would be able to assist other mem-

bers of the family. Particularly attractive to parents were middle-
level, white-collar careers such as accounting.

A follow-up study of ninth-grade graduates provided the first
hard evidence on what happened to students schooled under the
Reform. On the one hand, the findings were encouraging: over 85
percent of the students were continuing their education, and the
Reform was to some extent achieving its object of directing more
students into the diversified technical programs offered at the bachillerato level. On the other hand, half the students continuing their
education were enrolled in the traditional bachillerato programs
leading to the university, and thus apparently wanted professional
careers rather than the middle-level technical jobs the Reform's planners had wanted to promote.

The follow-up analysis, together with other aspiration data, also
revealed that conditions were tending to encourage the increased
migration of Third Cycle graduates to El Salvador's cities. In fact,
about half the graduates who were able to continue their education
had to leave the town in which they had finished ninth grade and
commute, or move to, a larger town. This trend may call for a policy of placing new schools outside the urban areas. The considerably
higher proportion of rural graduates who were neither working nor
studying and the lower proportion of rural students among full-time
students also emphasize the poorer educational opportunities of the
rural Salvadorean student.

In the final analysis, the students' high educational aspirations and
expectations were not surprising in a country where schooling is
still regarded as a sure passport to success and social mobility. When
access to higher education is limited, its value and attraction may
become exaggerated. This seems to be what has occurred in El Salvador.

El Salvador's universities are not likely to expand at a rate that
will satisfy the aspirations of the many Third Cycle students. Given
the government's plan to make nine grades of basic schooling available to all children, entrance to the prestigious bachillerato level may
also become more exclusive, despite the Reform's attempts to expand and diversify education at that level. It must be concluded,
therefore, that the high educational aspirations of students are not

realistic in terms of the tangible opportunities available to them in the near future.

If, as the evidence suggests, students are unrealistic in their assessment of their own chances for obtaining higher education and the most prestigious professional jobs, an important task for El Salvador's educational planners in the coming years will be to help students readjust their personal aspirations and adapt to the realities and needs of their society. With their ambitious and far-reaching Educational Reform, the Salvadoreans have expanded opportunity and improved the efficiency of their educational system; but they do not seem, as yet, to have encouraged young people to think about alternative forms of technical training and employment.

CHAPTER SIX

Teachers, Television, and Educational Reform

The original advocates of instructional television in El Salvador were not educators but businessmen and merchants, most of whom had little confidence in their country's public school system. With an effective ITV service, they hoped to compensate for what they considered an inadequately trained and poorly motivated corps of classroom teachers by shifting major responsibility to the more expert television teachers. In the new system, classroom teachers would assume a more passive monitoring role. Their prime duties would be the maintenance of classroom discipline and the faithful execution of instructions issued by the teleteachers.

The actual planners of the Reform within the Ministry of Education objected vigorously to these views, which they considered naive. If ITV and the other Reform programs were to succeed, they argued, classroom teachers would have to shoulder more, not less, responsibility. In fact, they felt the Reform would inevitably fail without the full cooperation and understanding of all classroom personnel. In 1969-72, accordingly, a major effort was made to retrain all Third Cycle teachers and to assist them in the implementation of the new policies.

These classroom teachers were the focus of an extensive research effort by the ITV evaluation team. Teachers' attitudes toward ITV and the Reform, toward the problems of schooling, and toward teaching as a profession were carefully monitored. This study was supplemented in 1969 and 1970 by surveys of teachers in retraining. In addition, classroom teaching was observed in the field during 1970. The results of all these studies are reported in this chapter.

THE TEACHER RETRAINING PROGRAM

Recognizing the key role of teachers in the Reform, the Ministry of Education undertook a comprehensive and costly retraining program as a corollary to the adoption of television. By 1973, virtually all Third Cycle teachers had been retrained at the refurbished San Andrés normal school, also the site of the first ITV production studio. They received advanced training in their subject specialties, as well as instruction in new teaching methods (including ITV utilization), student guidance, and evaluation. The program provided full salaries for all teachers in retraining, besides providing substitute teachers in the schools. No other country has made such an extensive effort to prepare its teachers when introducing ITV.

The first retraining course, during the three vacation months preceding the start of the 1969 school year, was organized for the teachers assigned to the 32 pilot ITV classes. The teachers who attended this and two subsequent vacation courses were enthusiastic about the Reform and ITV, and remained so during their first year in ITV classrooms. From 1969 through 1972, another four groups, of 250 teachers each, participated in full-year retraining courses at San Andrés. They, too, returned to their schools with generally positive attitudes toward the Reform and ITV, although the attitudes of each succeeding group were somewhat less favorable than those of its predecessors.

A special retraining course was organized at the end of 1969 for recent graduates of the Normal Superior, El Salvador's most prestigious secondary teacher training center. This course ran for three months, and the teachers enrolled in it were outspokenly critical of the Educational Reform, of ITV, and of the retraining course, which they considered a waste of time. Their bitterness toward the Ministry did not diminish with time, and they left San Andrés with the same negative attitudes.

CLASSROOM TEACHERS' ATTITUDES TOWARD ITV

As Figure 6.1 indicates, the teachers whose classes received ITV in 1969 were highly positive toward it at the end of the academic year. A large majority of them believed that the medium helped them enormously, although certain logistical and pedagogical difficulties

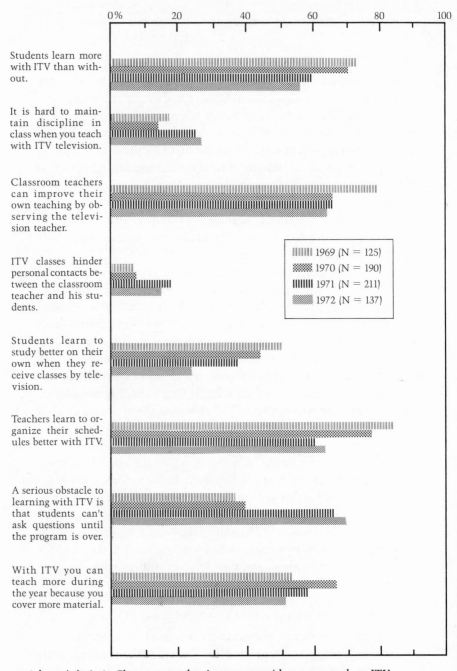

6.1 *(above & facing)*. Classroom teachers' agreement with statements about ITV

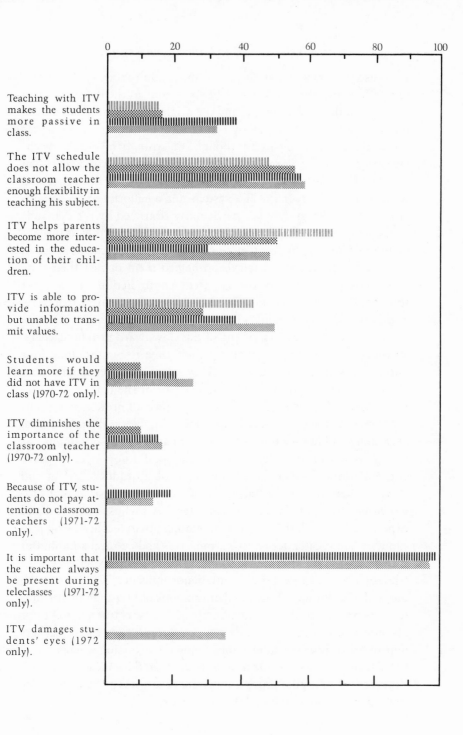

	0	20	40	60	80	100

Teaching with ITV makes the students more passive in class.

The ITV schedule does not allow the classroom teacher enough flexibility in teaching his subject.

ITV helps parents become more interested in the education of their children.

ITV is able to provide information but unable to transmit values.

Students would learn more if they did not have ITV in class (1970-72 only).

ITV diminishes the importance of the classroom teacher (1970-72 only).

Because of ITV, students do not pay attention to classroom teachers (1971-72 only).

It is important that the teacher always be present during teleclasses (1971-72 only).

ITV damages students' eyes (1972 only).

were also recognized as significant problems. In 1970, a second group of retrained teachers returned to the classroom, as the Reform spread throughout the seventh grade, and the original 32 pilot classes moved into eighth grade. A survey of 190 classroom teachers in that year revealed a disquieting pattern: though still strongly favorable, teachers were less positive toward ITV at the end of the second year than they had been at the end of the first. The sharpest criticism concerned the lack of flexibility in the ITV system, and a majority of the respondents indicated that they felt particularly restricted by the demands of the broadcast schedule. This finding must be interpreted in light of the fact that 77 percent of the same sample of teachers agreed with the proposition that television helped them budget their time more effectively. Despite the apparent contradiction in these responses, they prompted El Salvador's program planners to review more carefully the demands ITV was placing on classroom teachers.

To gain a better understanding of this downward turn in teachers' attitudes toward ITV, we analyzed their 1970 responses along four important background variables: (1) whether a teacher taught in an urban or a rural school; (2) what subjects he or she taught; (3) years of teaching experience with television; (4) level of professional training. The results were disappointing. Two variables, subject and level of training, did not seem to correlate with attitudes in any significant way. Assignment to a particular school, too, did not appear to have affected attitudes toward television, and the attitudes of urban and rural teachers were never far apart. We had hypothesized that ITV would be more popular among rural teachers, whose resources and experience were relativly poor, than among urban teachers, who presumably had greater access to learning aids and cultural stimuli. But there was only slight evidence of this phenomenon. Experience with television seemed to exert the only major influence. Teachers in the original pilot group retained higher opinions of ITV than their counterparts who entered the system in 1970. This was true on 10 of our attitude measures. And on only two measures ("Classroom teachers improve their own teaching by observing the television teacher," and "ITV helps parents become more interested in the education of their children") did the pilot group express markedly less positive attitudes toward television than it had the year before.

Tuition fees for Third Cycle students were eliminated in 1971, producing a sharp expansion in enrollment that created severe problems. Most schools went on double sessions, and teachers were therefore asked to assume extra duties. Incensed by these conditions, and feeling that their salary demands were being totally ignored by the Ministry, the leaders of El Salvador's powerful teachers' union, the Asociación Nacional de Educadores Salvadoreños (ANDES), called a general strike midway through the year. For some two months the schools either closed or carried on with reduced attendance. Even after a compromise settlement was reached, the teachers continued to express dissatisfaction with the Reform programs, and particularly with the rather high-handed manner in which many of these had been introduced. Thus the schools were in disarray for months, and hostile feelings between ANDES and the Ministry persisted long after the strike. In addition, many teachers had to be transferred to different communities because local parents resented their personal participation in the strike. Given all these difficulties, it is hardly surprising that our survey showed teacher attitudes toward ITV to be much more critical in 1971 than they had been in previous years; and most observers felt that the strike was the chief reason for this.

We awaited the results of the attitude survey conducted in November 1972, at the end of the fourth year of research, with more than usual interest. Would teachers' attitudes toward ITV and the Reform remain negative, or would they return to the highly favorable levels of 1969 and 1970? Whether as a lingering result of the strike or simply as evidence of a progressive disenchantment with ITV, teachers' attitudes in 1972 proved to be about the same as they had been in 1971.

What the teachers said about ITV must be seen in perspective. They became progressively less inclined to believe that students could learn more with ITV; but even at the end of 1972 more than half of them still held this view, and 63 percent of them still believed that classroom teachers could improve their own teaching by observing the teleteachers. Only 15 percent believed that ITV undermined their relationship with their students. The decline in positive attitudes was certainly there, but the majority of teachers still gave positive responses to most of our statements.

On one measure, results remained disappointing throughout the years of the study. In spite of retraining and increasing familiarity with ITV, the old fear that television might damage students' eyes—so often denied by experts and never really supported by evidence—was retained by 35 percent of the teachers in 1972, the last year attitudes were measured. The same belief was held by more than half the students, however, and it was particularly widespread in El Salvador's rural areas.

ATTITUDES TOWARD TEACHING AND EDUCATION
IN EL SALVADOR

Besides investigating the teachers' attitudes toward the ITV program in particular, the survey team monitored their opinions on teaching in general, on El Salvador's educational system and policies,

TABLE 6.1
*Teachers' Agreement with Statements About Teaching and
Education in El Salvador*

	Percent agreeing		
Statements	1970 (N = 190)	1971 (N = 213)	1972 (N = 137)
Teaching is not a very satisfying profession	18%	27%	37%
All young people should have the opportunity to finish Third Cycle	98	97	94
The recent increase in enrollment decreases the quality of secondary education	36	55	55
The fundamental goal of education is the formation of a child's character	71	74	58
I would encourage my best students to become teachers	20	13	20
Only the best students should study beyond primary	4	8	7
Teachers are highly respected in El Salvador	18	13	16
The majority of Third Cycle students are not very interested in learning	29	33	46
I would stay in teaching even if I were offered a better-paying job	45	33	34
Many students lack respect for their teachers	48	43	65
The most important goal of education is the development of reasoning ability	68	72	54
The great majority of students want to take advantage of their Third Cycle education	71	47	34
The Educational Reform is leading toward a high quality of Third Cycle education	48	53	46

and on the various changes imposed by the Reform. The collection of these data began in November 1970, after the Reform had been applied in a significant number of Salvadorean classrooms, and after the small pilot group of retrained teachers had been reinforced by the graduates of later training programs.

At the end of each school year the teachers in our sample were asked to agree or disagree with a number of statements about their work, choosing their responses from five alternatives (neutral, agree or disagree, and completely agree or disagree). Table 6.1 shows the percentage of each sample agreeing with the statements in whole or in part. In addition, we wanted to measure the teachers' own feelings about a number of problems that the research team, for one reason or another, considered important in El Salvador. Respondents were presented with a problem that might be present in their own class-room or in the nation's educational system as a whole and were asked to rate it as "insignificant," "minor," "serious," or "very serious." In this case we were concerned chiefly with the percentage who felt that a problem was very serious (Table 6.2).

The statements and problems in Tables 6.1 and 6.2 were presented to all three samples. By 1972, however, we were especially interested in teachers' thoughts about several points that had been raised dur-

TABLE 6.2
Teachers' Perceptions of "Very Serious" Problems in Teaching and the Educational System

Problem	Percent rating as "very serious"		
	1970 (N = 190)	1971 (N = 213)	1972 (N = 137)
Financial position of teachers	54%	55%	42%
Poverty of students and their surroundings	45	49	44
Shortage of teachers with a real gift for teaching	34	29	35
Lack of teaching materials	34	43	40
Lack of cooperation from parents	27	32	38
Too many students in class	26	39	44
Efficiency of the Ministry of Education	22	27	23
Methods of assigning teachers to schools	21	35	31
Guides and workbooks do not arrive on time	14	29	28
Administration within the schools	11	14	13
Lack of supervision from Ministry of Education	10	9	15
Technical failures in the reception of teleclasses	8	15	12
Student behavior in class	—	9	18

ing and after the 1971 teachers' strike; and we could feel confident that more teachers were acquainted with the Reform programs and the government's implementation of them. We therefore offered our 1972 sample of 137 teachers a number of additional statements and problems for consideration.

In 1971 El Salvador had replaced the old standards for promotion to higher grades with the new system of "oriented" promotion, which moved students on to the next grade unless they showed severe deficiencies in attendance and performance. This policy required a good deal more evaluation and supervision by classroom teachers than the single passing examination administered under the traditional system. And by 1972 it had moved extra students on to the higher grades of the Third Cycle, increasing the enrollment pressure that had begun when tuition was eliminated the preceding year. Most of our added statements for 1972 dealt with this new policy:

> The idea of oriented promotion will be good for the educational system of El Salvador (30% agreement).
> Oriented promotion in no way diminishes the quality of Salvadorean education (36%).
> Teachers are sufficiently informed about methods of scholastic evaluation to be able to implement oriented promotion in their classes (24%).
> Teachers are having no difficulty in implementing oriented promotion (18%).
> Oriented promotion does not in any way diminish students' interest in their studies (19%).
> The new curricula of the Third Cycle aim at producing the type of graduate that El Salvador truly needs (54%).
> The new curricula are of more help to the classroom teacher than the curricula of previous years (77%).

If anything, 1971-72 was a period of problems for Salvadorean education. The following difficulties we mentioned were considered "very serious" by the indicated percentages of our 1972 sample:

Lack of desks (50%).
Lack of reference materials and learning aids for students (48%).

Lack of communication between the Ministry of Education and
the teachers (37%).
Physical condition of the classrooms (26%).
Too few television receivers (25%).
Lack of knowledge of the techniques necessary for evaluating
student performance (22%).
Quality of teleclasses (12%).
Content of student workbooks (9%).

We also asked the teachers to name serious problems that had not
been included in our own list. Three problems were mentioned by a
significant percentage of the sample:

Lack of resources in the classroom (22%).
Lack of coordination between various Ministry branches (e.g.,
ETV, Supervision, Normal School) (12%).
No specified division of responsibilities between classroom and
TV teachers (11%).

Taking all the survey results together, it is obvious that these were
not very happy teachers. In two years, the percentage of teachers
who felt that teaching was not a satisfying profession doubled (Table
6.1). Only a minority of the sample ever felt that teachers were highly
respected in El Salvador, or said that they would encourage their
best students to become teachers. And there was growing dissatisfaction with classroom conditions, student attitudes, and the overall
capability of the Ministry to carry through with the Reform programs.

It was not that teachers disagreed with the basic goals of El Salvador's Educational Reform. Over the period of evaluation, almost all
continued to agree that all young people ought to have the opportunity to finish the Third Cycle (though this was the policy responsible for increased enrollments and heavier teaching loads). They
also gave a vote of confidence to the new curricula, and a majority
of them felt that these would be able to produce the kind of Third
Cycle graduates that El Salvador needed. ITV, too, was generally
considered a worthwhile innovation. It was the teachers' own job
satisfaction that declined.

The problems that teachers listed as "very serious" were illuminating. In the early years, the financial position of teachers was the problem cited most often. It was still high on the list in 1972 (42 percent), but no longer the major problem. The most serious problems that year were the lack of desks, the lack of reference materials, overcrowded classes, and the general poverty of students and their surroundings. Two of the general attitude responses fit closely with this list: a steadily increasing percentage of teachers agreed that the majority of Third Cycle students were not very interested in learning; and a steadily decreasing percentage felt that most students wanted to take advantage of their education in the Third Cycle.

Despite the classroom teachers' strong belief in universal education through the ninth grade, they resented the demands put on them by the enormous increases in enrollment this policy entailed. By 1972, most schools were on two shifts, and even so many classes had more than 50 students. Consequently, there were often too few desks, textbooks, and reference materials to go around. Students in large, poorly equipped classes taught by overworked teachers were not likely to be highly motivated—or to generate much enthusiasm among their teachers. Another source of frustration was the new system of oriented promotion. Instead of passing or failing students entirely on the basis of a single, teacher-constructed examination given at the end of the school year, teachers now had to evaluate their performance throughout the year; similarly, students had to keep up their studies throughout the year rather than cram for the crucial examination. The advantages of the new system were that the evaluation of students was far more comprehensive, and that the number of repeaters and dropouts would be markedly reduced. But many teachers did not feel confident of their own ability to keep up a continuing evaluation. Moreover, decreasing the importance of the final examination did take away some of the students' motivation to study hard and to be attentive and respectful in class; after all, they expected to pass anyway.

To sum up, the responses to our survey indicated that a large number of problems were responsible for the teachers' depressed attitudes. The salary issue was especially acute, and was compounded by swelling enrollments and overworked teachers. There was general

Teaching with television

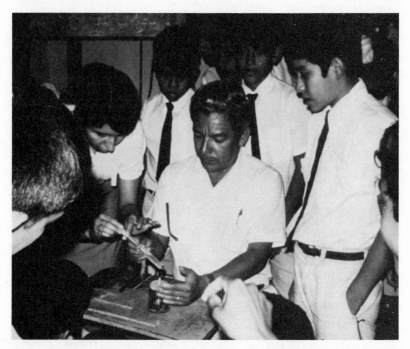

Following the broadcast of a science lesson, the classroom teacher goes over
the material and answers questions (*Henry T. Ingle*)

Student science projects at an exposition sponsored by the Ministry of Education
in 1970; the traditional system of education in El Salvador did not encourage
such activities

confusion over the part to be played by the classroom teacher in the new system of evaluation and promotion, which was in addition viewed as a threat to the teacher's authority in the classroom. And there were many long-standing grievances against the Ministry: poor administration, inaccessibility, lack of coordination, late arrival or shortage of teaching materials, devious methods of assigning teachers to schools, and so forth. Obviously, much of the Salvadorean teachers' negative feeling was justified.

In an independent study of the bitter strike that overshadowed all other educational activities in 1971, a research team from the Universidad Centroamericana José Simeón Cañas accurately portrayed the frustration and sense of betrayal shared by many teachers during this period:

> The current Ministry's emphasis on the expansion and restructuring of the educational system and on the incorporation of new technological devices in the teaching process contrast notably with its air of neglect and disdain for the human needs of teachers. . . . Considering this disregard of the teachers' plight, and the hostile reaction of their union, it is illogical to claim there has been any genuine qualitative reform of Salvadorean education. Such disregard is still a major shortcoming of the current Ministry; and it contributed markedly to the teachers' exasperation and sense of alienation . . . when individual frustration was converted to group solidarity.[1]

TEACHERS' RATINGS OF THE TELEVISED COURSES

For three years (1970-72), we asked classroom teachers to rate the quality and effectiveness of each ITV lesson series on various feedback questionnaires (see Appendix C).[2] The most abrupt change revealed by this study was the sudden demise of televised mathematics, which began in 1970 as the most highly rated course in the seventh-grade series and the second most highly rated in the eighth

---

[1] Universidad Centroamericana "José Simeón Cañas," *Análisis de una experiencia nacional* (San Salvador: Editorial Lea, 1971), p. 116.

[2] The questionnaires were administered approximately one month before the end of each school year. Teacher samples were stratified according to the individual teleseries and were drawn independently from the larger samples of teachers who participated in each year-end attitude study. In place of the positive and negative statements used to elicit attitudes toward ITV, these questionnaires used neutral phrases regarding 20 varying aspects of the television classes and their results.

TABLE 6.3
*Teachers' Preferences for Number of Classroom
Periods with ITV, 1972*

Subject	Percent favoring		
	All periods with ITV	No change	No ITV
Mathematics	12%	62%	26%
Science	32	63	5
Social studies	33	64	3
English	48	47	5
Spanish	22	69	9

NOTE: $N = 137$; however, not all respondents expressed an opinion on every course.

grade. By 1972 it was at the bottom of the list in all three grades. Over the same period, Spanish and social studies emerged as the most effective courses in teachers' eyes.

In 1972 teachers also were asked, with reference to each course, whether they would prefer to have television in all class periods, in the number of periods presently broadcast (usually three per week), or in fewer periods. In a sense, this was a more reliable judgment than a simple quality rating, since it represented teachers' estimates of the real usefulness of each course (see Table 6.3).

Teachers favored an expansion of ITV lessons in English more than in any other subject. Most remarked that ITV helped them especially in conducting oral drills with the language. Accordingly, about half of them voted to extend televised English classes to all periods, as compared to one out of three who wanted that much social studies and science, and one out of five who wanted that much Spanish. A second significant finding was that very few teachers wished to see the amount of televised instruction reduced: even in mathematics, three-fourths of the sample wanted at least the same number of tele-classes per week.

TEACHING STYLES AND CLASSROOM INTERACTION

In a pilot study undertaken in 1970, an observation form was developed to help Salvadorean school supervisors evaluate classroom teaching behavior, to point up differences between teachers, and to assess the progress of individual teachers toward the adoption of

modern teaching methods.[3] The observation method itself was derived from the work of the New Zealand educator C. E. Beeby.[4]
Beeby's guiding hypothesis is that educational systems evolve through
four stages, and that the general education and professional preparation of teachers is directly related to these stages. Teachers in the
first stage ("dame school") are poorly educated and have little training. When they gain some professional experience in their craft,
they tend to move into stage two ("formalism"), in which classroom
methods are closely tied to the content of an official syllabus. With
still more education comes stage three ("transition"); and by stage
four ("meaning") teachers are well educated, highly trained, and
able to respond creatively to the unique learning needs of each student.

Although the study was undertaken primarily to develop and test
an observation form for use by Salvadoreans themselves, it also revealed a number of important differences between ITV and non-ITV
classrooms that were of use to our main evaluation project. First,
the introduction of classroom television and the written materials
that accompanied the broadcasts sharply reduced teachers' dictation in the Reform classrooms. Traditional teachers dictated six times
as much as teachers in ITV classrooms, spending, on the average,
over 20 percent of the observed class time reading from a book while
students copied the material verbatim. Second, teachers in ITV classrooms asked more than twice as many open-ended or "thought"
questions as their non-ITV counterparts, and students volunteered
their own opinions much more frequently. Third, several different
innovative learning aids (e.g. live animals, or homemade maps and
science equipment) were utilized in the ITV classrooms, whereas not
one such learning aid was observed in the traditional classrooms.
Finally, students were observed working in groups in several ITV
classes, but never in a non-ITV class.

All 16 Salvadorean teachers observed were classified in Beeby's
second stage on the basis of classroom performance. However, an

---

[3] The study was conducted by Judith Allen Mayo, who also wrote the initial
draft of this section. See Appendix C for observation form.

[4] C. E. Beeby, *The quality of education in developing countries* (Cambridge,
Mass.: Harvard University Press, 1968).

examination of the school records of these teachers revealed no significant correlations between that performance and their years of education and training. Indeed, some of the non-ITV teachers had received more schooling and more advanced training than their ITV counterparts; yet the evidence indicated that the latter were teaching in a more modern way. One important background characteristic separating the two groups was the year-long course of orientation, retraining, and teaching practice that the ITV teachers had received under the Educational Reform. Could a single year of retraining make such a difference? It was clear that neither group of teachers had learned up-to-date methods in their normal schools; nor had they been well instructed in their subject specialties. These findings did not really undermine Beeby's hypothesis regarding the importance of general education and teacher training in the modernization of teaching behavior. Rather, they suggested that if change is desired, additional abstract training is not enough: teachers must also be encouraged to practice the methods they will be expected to use in their own classrooms later on.

The Educational Reform was clearly beginning to introduce some techniques of modern pedagogy into the classrooms of El Salvador. In Beeby's terms, Salvadorean teachers were moving gradually away from their "formalistic" reliance on traditional methods. However, the results of the pilot observation study also suggested that describing changes in teaching in terms of four discrete stages did not adequately reflect the complexity of the development process.

The Third Cycle teachers in El Salvador did not seem to be making dramatic innovations. Though all 16 of the teachers observed could be classified as "second stage," they were clearly at different levels within that stage. Progress seemed to occur in tiny steps, and it was slow and uneven. Teachers in ITV classes did seem to be moving away from a reliance on rote learning, however, and toward the more individualized, problem-solving learning that was the goal of the Educational Reform. Apparently minor changes may have been more significant than the numbers suggest. For example, when compared to teachers who asked no open-ended questions, the teachers who posed even one such question per class had changed more significantly than the difference between "zero" and "one" suggests. The adoption of a previously nonexistent technique in the classroom was probably much more important than increasing the use of an established one.

OBSERVATION OF TWO CLASSROOMS

In 1972, our efforts to understand the local and individual effects of the Reform, which had begun in 1970 with the development of the teacher observation form, were extended through a study of how the Reform actually looked in the classroom and what impact it was having on the individual lives of Salvadorean children. A detailed case study was made of two seventh-grade classrooms (one rural and one urban) that had received ITV for the first time in 1972.[5] Among the research instruments employed were direct teacher-student classroom observations, in-depth interviews, home visits, sociograms, and written learning and attitudinal measures. Daily records of classroom events were maintained throughout the year, and the observer paid frequent visits to the communities and homes of students.

Insofar as it related to teachers, this study revealed various instances of teachers' inability to cope with student discipline or with certain subjects, inconsistency in the use of new and old teaching styles, and a tendency for some teachers to prefer "going it alone" without ITV. In general, however, four years of the Reform had increased the confidence of classroom teachers and had made them more demanding critics of the televised lessons. The study results also showed an interesting pattern suggesting that at least two of the three key elements of the ITV system—teleteacher, classroom teacher, and subject matter—had to be highly valued by students if the system as a whole was to perform well in the classroom. In this context, the classroom teacher would appear to be capable of greatly enhancing or weakening the effectiveness of televised instruction.

SUMMARY AND IMPLICATIONS

El Salvador's Educational Reform made a concerted effort to retrain all Third Cycle teachers so that they could work effectively with the revised curriculum and the new ITV system. During our research

[5] This study was conducted by Yolanda Ingle.

between 1969 and 1972, teachers' attitudes toward ITV, though remaining generally positive, became steadily more critical as the Reform programs had interacted to produce many changes, the program of teacher retraining was perhaps most crucial to the success of ITV in El Salvador's classrooms.

The teachers' ratings of individual ITV series over the four years showed a changing pattern of preferences: mathematics declined in all three grades, whereas Spanish and social studies improved. When asked how much televised instruction they wanted in the different subjects, 25 percent of the math teachers and very few other teachers favored cutting television back. Most teachers wanted about the same amount of televised instruction as before (3 classes per week), although 50 percent of the English teachers preferred to have all classes with television.

Our project to develop and validate a form for observing classroom teaching behavior, based on Beeby's theory of development stages in teaching, permitted researchers and school supervisors to distinguish modern from traditional teaching behaviors. The results of evaluating a sample of 16 teachers with the form showed that whereas years of formal training did not seem to affect classroom behavior, teachers retrained under the Reform were gradually adopting more modern teaching techniques. An intensive study of two classrooms concluded that teachers' self-confidence had increased, and that classroom teachers had become more demanding critics of televised instruction in the course of the Reform. These two observation studies, taken together, implied that although the various Reform programs had interacted to produce many changes, the program of teacher retraining was perhaps most crucial to the success of ITV and the introduction of modern pedagogy to El Salvador's classrooms.

These results permit some generalizations about Salvadorean teachers and their reactions to television. The observational evidence indicated that Salvadorean teachers were beginning to rely less on lecturing or rote drill and more on student activity; they were asking more "thought" questions (that is, questions with no single correct answer), and they were encouraging students to ask their own questions, state their own opinions, and work on individual projects.

These techniques were all observed frequently enough to suggest that classroom teachers were changing, but that they still had far to go if the Reform's ambitious goals were to be achieved.

As for teachers' specific reactions to television, perhaps the best way to sum up the results would be to say that much of the enthusiasm of 1969 had faded by the end of 1972. Nevertheless, both teachers' and students' attitudes remained predominantly favorable to the use of ITV; and, despite disagreement with Ministry officials on the way some changes had been implemented, teachers were in accord with the basic ideas and philosophy of the Reform.

Did the downward trend in teachers' attitudes during the Reform's first four years belie the wisdom of spending so much time and money on their retraining? That depends on how legitimate one considers the teachers' grievances. The problem may not have been ITV or the Reform so much as the low pay and poor working conditions (larger class sizes, grueling double sessions, and lack of classroom materials) that teachers had to live with. Given these handicaps, it was not surprising that the teachers were dissatisfied enough to strike.

The year's retraining unquestionably sharpened the teachers' skills; it may also have raised their consciousness to the point where they were able to criticize ITV and the other reforms when these were not of adequate quality or did not serve their interests. In the final analysis, the teachers did not fear or resent ITV, but they did become increasingly aware of its shortcomings. And insofar as they were critical of specific television series, their criticisms were often justified.

Our results also suggest that if teachers are expected to use modern methods in their daily teaching, they must first be carefully instructed in those methods and allowed to practice them. The effectiveness of televised instruction depends largely on the cooperation and resourcefulness of the classroom teacher. A mediocre TV lesson can be made effective through good classroom utilization, just as a good television lesson can be weakened by poor utilization. Neither the classroom teacher nor television can be expected to maintain a consistently high level of performance, and each will have good and bad days. In combination, however, ITV and the classroom teacher can reinforce one another and enhance the quality of learning.

CHAPTER SEVEN

The Cost of ITV

As part of the evaluation of ITV in El Salvador, Richard E. Speagle published a detailed analysis of the system's costs in 1972.[1] This chapter provides an updated analysis of those costs, using Speagle's data as a departure point. The first part of the chapter outlines the methodology that guided the analysis of ITV's costs. In the second part, the major results of this endeavor are presented. Finally, a number of factors that partially offset the add-on cost of ITV in El Salvador are discussed.

METHODOLOGY OF THE COST STUDY

The analysis followed a standard approach in dividing ITV costs into three categories: program production, transmission, and reception. The expenditures incurred for each year in each category were then arrayed in a cost tableau. Wherever possible, historical data were incorporated to fill in the cost tableau, and planning projections were made for future years. It was then possible to construct total, average, and marginal cost functions, and to estimate the average cost incurred per student-year of ITV use. Because so many of the expenses of ITV in El Salvador were funded by foreign grants and loans, it was also important to distinguish between total costs and costs borne solely by the government of El Salvador.

[1] The original draft of this chapter was written by Dr. Dean Jamison of the Educational Testing Service, Princeton, N.J. Cf. Richard E. Speagle, *Educational reform and instructional television in El Salvador: Costs, benefits, and payoffs* (Washington, D.C.: Academy for Educational Development, 1972).

Total, Average, and Marginal Cost

It is useful to think of costs as functions rather than numbers. A total cost function for a particular educational resource or input portrays the total cost required to finance that input as a function of the amount of input required. Taking ITV as an example, let total cost function = $T(N)$, where $T(N)$ is the total cost required to provide an input of ITV to N students.

The average cost function (i.e. the unit cost function) equals the total cost function divided by the number of units of input provided. Thus average cost = $A = A(N) = T(N)/N$. Just as the total cost depends on N, so may the average cost.

The marginal cost function is the additional cost of providing ITV to one more student than the number of students already served.[2] Thus marginal cost = $M(n+1) = T(n+1) - T(N)$. Again, it is important to remember that marginal cost is generally a function of N.

When the total cost function can be approximated in a simple and convenient linear form, it is possible to distinguish between fixed and variable costs:

[1] $$T(N) = F + VN$$

Here, F is the fixed cost because its contribution to total cost is independent of N; V is the variable cost because its contribution to total cost varies directly with N. Given such a linear total cost function, the average cost function is simply $F/N + V$. And the marginal cost function is equal to V. Thus the average cost decline as N increases (spreading the fixed cost over more units), and when N is very large, the average cost is close to the marginal cost. In this case, A/V is only slightly larger than 1. On the other hand, a large A/V means that the fixed costs have not been spread over many students. A/V, then, is a good measure of the extent to which economies of scale have been realized in a system.

Equation 1 reflects the cost behavior of most ITV systems. Program preparation and transmission tend to be independent of the number of students using the system, and thus constitute the major

---

[2] As usually stated, the marginal cost function is the derivative of the total cost function.

part of the fixed cost, F. Reception costs, by contrast, vary directly with the number of students, and are thus included in V. In order to apply Equation 1, values for F and V must be estimated empirically. This means that capital costs (e.g. studios) must be combined with recurrent costs (e.g. teachers' salaries) in some appropriate way. A capital cost is one incurred in purchasing something that will have a useful lifetime extending beyond the time of purchase. Recurrent costs, on the other hand, are incurred for goods or services that are used up as they are bought. The principal cost of school systems is the recurrent cost of teachers' time; and the useful lifetime of their service simply coincides with the pay period. The line between capital and recurrent costs is usually drawn at one year—that is, if the useful lifetime of a piece of equipment is greater than one year, it is treated as a capital cost. School systems may adhere only loosely to this convention, however.[3]

Occasionally, confusion also arises over just what are fixed versus capital costs. Some fixed costs can be recurrent, like that of the electric power required to operate a television transmitter. And some capital costs may be variable, such as the number of television receivers purchased for local use. Although fixed and capital costs are conceptually distinct, then, it is often true that major capital expenditures are associated with substantial fixed costs.

How does one construct the cost function of Equation 1 if capital costs are present? Jamison and Klees have described a method that prorates the capital cost by year and adds it to the yearly recurrent cost.[4] Two key variables are involved. The first is the lifetime of capital equipment: if it lasts n years, a fraction of its cost (on the average, $1/n$) should be charged to each year as equipment depreciation. The second variable is the social discount rate—essentially a value judgment of the cost of withdrawing resources from present consumption in order to have something of value in the future. Values used for the social discount rate are expressed as annual rates of interest similar to, though often lower than, private rates of interest.

[3] See P. Coombs and J. Hallak, *Managing educational costs* (New York: Oxford University Press, 1972), chap. 9.

[4] See D. Jamison and S. Klees, "The cost of instructional radio and television for developing countries. *Instructional Science*, 1975, no. 4, pp. 333-84.

(The rate for the El Salvador study, 7.5 percent, is a value typically used in development planning.) If one is given an initial cost, C, for an item of capital equipment, its lifetime, n, and the social discount rate, r, the annualized cost of the capital may be defined as $a(r,n)C$. To calculate the annualization factor, $a(r,n)$, the following equation is employed:

[2] $$a(r,n) = [r(1+r)]^n/[(1+r)^n - 1]$$

In the El Salvador analysis, $r = .075$, and the value of n varied according to the nature of the capital equipment considered.

By using Equation 2 to convert capital costs into annual fixed costs, we could estimate the parameters F and V of the function portrayed in Equation 1 and could also compensate for the uneven distribution of capital expenditures across time. However, Salvadorean students' use of television during the course of the Reform was also uneven—low at the outset and high later. For this reason it was important to introduce a notion of average cost that incorporated utilization data as well as expenditure data.[5]

Computation of Average Cost

We needed to display the unit costs of ITV in El Salvador's Educational Reform in a way that took explicit account of the time structure of classroom utilization and also permitted costs to be examined from a number of time perspectives. The last point was critical. At the outset, the government had to invest heavily in order to buy equipment, develop TV production, and start up operations in the schools. Three or four years later the cost picture was very different indeed: initial capital costs had sunk, and, except for the potential resale value of equipment, there was nothing to be recovered from abandoning the ITV project. What the situation demanded, therefore, was a method for calculating costs from the perspective of a decision-maker at various times before and during the project.

It was also desirable to consider various time horizons for El Salvador. What would the average cost have been if ITV had been aban-

---

[5] Dividing Equation 1 by N gives the average cost associated with a particular value of N. But since N varies with time (generally increasing as the system matures), it is desirable to obtain an average cost that accounts for this.

doned after five years? After 15 years? This problem underscored the importance of looking at average costs from year i of the project onward through year j.[6] The average cost from i to j is denoted by A_{ij}, and is defined as the total expenditure on the project between years i and j divided by total use of the project (i.e. number of students), with both costs and use discounted back to year i by the social discount rate, r. Let C_k be equal to the total amount to be spent on the project in year k, seen either as fixed and variable costs or as capital and recurrent costs. Let N_k be the total number of students using the system in the same year. Then

$$[3] \qquad A_{ij} = \frac{\sum\limits_{K=i}^{j} C_k/(1+r)^{k-i}}{\sum\limits_{K=i}^{j} N_k/(1+r)^{k-i}}$$

Since a decision-maker at the beginning of year i can in no way influence costs and use before that date, these are not incorporated in A_{ij}. What A_{ij} does provide is the cost per student of continuing the project through year j, assuming j to be the final year of the project. By examining how A_{ij} behaves as j varies, a decision-maker can estimate how long a project must continue for unit costs to fall to the desired point. When considering whether a particular project should be undertaken in the first place, he should let $i = 1$ (i.e., he should compute A_{1j} for various values of j to see how long it will take before the cost per student is a reasonable one). And once into a project, he should use the value of i corresponding to his present position in time.

Our cost analysis of ITV in El Salvador calculated average cost estimates for many values of i and j, holding the social discount rate

---

[6] It may be useful here to explain the concept of "present value" of a cost. Assume that a cost of $4,000 is to be incurred eight years from now. The present value of that cost is the amount that would have to be put aside now, at interest, to aggregate the $4,000 after eight years. If the annual interest rate is 6 percent, and if we put aside z dollars now, in eight years we will have $z(1.06)^8$, assuming annual compounding. The present value of $4,000 eight years hence, then, is $z = 4,000/(1.06)^8 = \$2,509.65$. The numerator of Equation 3 is the present value incurred between years i and j. The denominator is the present value of student utilization.

(r) constant at 7.5 percent. The A_{ij} values were also calculated for both total costs and costs borne exclusively by the Salvadorean government. It should be kept in mind that A_{ij} is a concept separate from that of average cost function, $A(N)$, discussed earlier. $A(N)$ indicates what the average cost would be for a given value of N, under the assumption that N remains the same from year to year. $A(N)$ is thus a measure of monetary cost only, not of actual utilization or derived benefit; and its value is an overall summary measure of unit cost. A_{ij}, however, is a measure based on actual (and projected) costs and utilization viewed from and to specific points in time. A_{ij} takes special account of the student utilization pattern over time.

Grants, Loans, and Loan Repayment

Since El Salvador received large foreign grants and loans to help finance her ITV system, the actual expenditures of the Salvadorean government were substantially less than the project's total costs. In order to adjust total costs for grants, one simply subtracts the amount of the grant in a given year from the total costs of that year. Loans, however, must be paid back at some point. The loans negotiated by El Salvador had a ten-year grace period before repayment was to commence. Thus in calculating costs for the early years of ITV we were able to treat loans like grants and simply subtract them from total costs to estimate total government costs; after ten years loan payments falling due in a given year had to be added to the total costs in order to obtain the system's overall cost to the government.

Computing the real cost of the payments was complicated by uncertainties about the future inflation rate of the dollar. When our cost estimate was compiled, we used a rough estimate of 4 percent; but at the time of this writing (1975) it is obvious that dollar inflation is probably unpredictable as little as several months into the future, let alone ten years. It is true that the Salvadorean *colon*, like most currencies elsewhere in the world, has recently been inflating at a rate far in excess of 4 percent. But the original ITV loans were negotiated in fixed dollar terms; and by 1980, when the first loan payments fall due, they will surely be made in dollars far cheaper

TABLE 7.1

Expenditures for ITV in Third Cycle Schools, 1966-88

(1,000's of 1972 U.S. dollars)

Category[a]	1966-67[b]	1968	1969	1970	1971	1972	1973	1974	1975	1976	1977
Production:											
Studios				234	108	36	36				
Equipment		50	270	40	966						
Operations			300	370	410	490	490	490	490	540	540
Start-up		380	360	260	210	200	200	100	50		
Videotape	100		51	51	51			51	51	51	
Transmission:											
Studios				26	12	4	4				
Equipment					644						
Operations			20	20	40	10	10	10	10	10	10
Reception:											
Equipment		1,140					53	62	80	13	13
Repl. and maintenance				120	120	120	50		120	120	120
Total cost	100	1,570	1,001	1,121	2,561	860	843	713	801	734	638
Grants and loans		−190	−680	−300	−1,980	−320	−320				
Total cost to government	100	1,380	321	821	581	540	523	713	801	734	638
Enrollment (1,000's)			2	14	32	48	60	72	86	104	107

a These costs were assigned as follows. *Production and transmission:* The costs of building the Santa Tecla studios were allocated 90 percent to production and 10 percent to transmission, with the air conditioning for the studios considered separately; video equipment costs were allocated 60 percent to production and 40 percent to transmission. The cost for videotape assumes a 5-year tape life, 300 hours of programming per year, and a price of $170 per hour-length reel. Start-up costs after 1974 are assumed to decrease over two years to $50,000, after which time they are included in the cost of operations. Through 1971, transmission costs are estimated at 25 percent of this figure. *Reception:* Beginning in 1973, this is based on the number of students and classrooms added to the system, assuming an average class size of 45 and a cost of $200 per TV receiver. The costs of classroom remodeling are included in this figure. *Grants and Loans:* The loans allow for a 10-year grace period before repayment, during which time interest accumulates at 2 percent annually. Repayment extends for the next 30 years, at 2.5 percent. Assuming a 4 percent annual inflation, the effective interest rates become −2 percent and −1.5 percent, respectively. Repayment is annualized as though the entire 40-year period for the loans began in 1970. *Enrollment:* The table assumes a rapid increase during 1972-76, after which a rate of roughly 3 percent per year is used, based on population growth. The most recent figures indicate that our estimates for the late 1970's may be as much as 10-15 percent too low.

b The only costs incurred before 1969 were those for pilot projects, planning studies, and other start-up procedures. The total cost given here is accurate, but exact allocation is impossible.

Table 7.1 (cont.)

Category[a]	1978	1979	1980	1981	1982	1983	1984	1985	1986	1987	1988
Production:											
Studios											
Equipment	50	270	36	36							
Operations	540	540	40	966	540	540	540	540	540	540	540
Videotape		51	540	540			51	51	51		
			51	51							
Transmission:											
Studios			4	4							
Equipment				644							
Operations	10	10	10	10	10	10	10	10	10	10	10
Reception:											
Equipment	13	18	13	18	18	18	13	18	18	22	18
Repl. and maintenance	103	62	200	133	133	116	80	213	151	151	134
Total cost	716	951	934	2,402	701	684	694	832	770	733	702
Grants and loans			45	45	45	45	45	45	45	45	45
Total cost to government	716	951	979	2,447	746	729	739	877	815	768	747
Enrollment (1,000's)	110	113	117	120	124	128	131	135	139	144	148

SOURCES: Cost data from Jamison and Klees, as originally presented in Speagle, *Educational reform*. Costs here do not include retraining of teachers, printing costs for teachers' manuals and student workbooks, or maintenance and power for reception equipment.

than those extrapolated by our cost analysis. Thus the costs to be borne by the Salvadorean government, as calculated in this chapter, are necessarily an overestimate (though by no more than roughly 5 percent). One must remember, however, that a Salvadorean decision-maker would have had no more information than our evaluation team did at the time of the survey, and would have had to base his plans on the same projected costs.

THE COST OF ITV

The methods just described were applied to the cost data gathered by Speagle, which are set forth in Table 7.1. Costs are listed in three subcategories: production, transmission, and reception. In the entries for foreign aid and debt repayment, negative numbers show the total amount of grant or loan money received in a particular year for the ITV system; in this case the amount is subtracted from total costs to give the cost to the government for the year. Beginning in 1980, the numbers in this row represent loan payments and were added to other costs. For convenience, Table 7.1 also gives past and projected student enrollment figures.

Program production costs exceeded the combined transmission and reception costs by a factor of two or three. A substantial fraction of these were capital costs, and it was important—particularly for the information of planners in other countries—to obtain an annualized estimate of total production costs, not just the yearly operating costs of program production. Table 7.2 presents the com-

TABLE 7.2
Costs of Program Production

Cost category	Amortization period	Cost	Annualized cost
Studio facility (building)	25 yr.	342	31
Studio facility (air conditioning)	10	72	10
Equipment	10	1,326	193
Start-up	25	1,860	167
Videotape	5	153	38
Operations (recurrent)	—	—	540
TOTAL			979

NOTE: Costs are expressed in thousands of 1972 dollars. The amortization period is the number of years the cost item is assumed to last; start-up costs are amortized over an assumed 25-year life for the project. The annualization was done using Equation 2, with a social discount rate of 7.5 percent per annum.

ponent and total costs of program production, including annualized capital expenditures at the 7.5 percent discount rate. The total production cost of $979,000 per year was almost twice the operations (i.e. recurrent) cost of $540,000 per year. At the estimated production rate of a thousand 20-minute programs per year, the cost per hour of program production in El Salvador came to about $2,940.

The Total Cost Function for ITV

Using the data from Table 7.1, it was also possible to obtain a cost function for ITV in El Salvador. The program production and transmission costs were considered fixed (the F component of Equation 1), and reception costs varied with the number of students (the V component of Equation 1). Start-up costs were treated as an initial capital investment and were annualized over the assumed 25-year lifetime of the ITV system. The 1972 student enrollment estimate of 48,000 was used, and we assumed an average of 170 hours of program presentation per grade per year; thus we could calculate values for A, for A/V, and for costs per student-hour of viewing (C_h). The values arrived at (in 1972 U.S. dollars) were as follows, assuming $r = 7.5$ percent:[7]

$$T(N) = \$1,116,000 + \$1.10N \qquad A/V = \$22.14$$
$$A = \$24.35 \qquad C_h = \$.143$$

With twice as many students using the system ($N = 96,000$), average costs fell to $12.73, and student-hour costs to $.075. The substantial reduction was possible because of the initially high value of A/V.

The total cost figure permitted the costs borne exclusively by the Salvadorean government to be computed. To do this, it was necessary to reduce the fixed-cost components by an annualized equivalent of the foreign grants and loans received. The present value of the 30-year loan repayment series was calculated and then subtracted from the total amount of the grants and loans (the total was assumed

[7] Jamison and Klees examined the sensitivity of the cost estimates to the value chosen for the social discount rate; increasing it from 7.5 percent to 15 percent increases A by about 20 percent. This substantial rise is due to the highly capital-intensive nature of the project.

to occur in 1970). The resulting figure was annualized over the assumed 25-year lifetime of the project and subtracted from fixed costs. The government costs were:

$$T(N) = \$799,000 + \$1.10N \qquad C_h = \$.104$$
$$A = \$17.75 \qquad\qquad A/V = \$16.13$$

The grants and loans obviously contributed substantially to the development of the ITV system. In fact, at the 7.5 percent social discount rate foreign contributions met approximately 27 percent of the system's total cost when 48,000 students were using it. Because the cost of expanding the system will eventually be borne entirely by El Salvador, the percentage of foreign contribution will decline as enrollments increase; owing to the high value of A/V, however, foreign assistance will account for more than 25 percent of total costs even after the enrollment passes 100,000 (projected for 1976).[8]

True Average Cost of ITV

The cost equations just given provide a reasonably clear picture of ITV costs as a function of the number of students per year using the system. In order to measure the actual average costs incurred, we also had to incorporate the time structure of student usage by computing values for A_{ij}.

The data in Table 7.1 were used to calculate values for the years 1966-88. Letting 1966 equal year 1, Equation 3 was used to compute all possible values of A_{ij} both for total costs and for costs borne exclusively by the Salvadorean government. (The results depended, of course, on the accuracy of the enrollment projections in the last row of Table 7.1, and deviations from these projections would induce corresponding deviations in average costs.) Figure 7.1 displays the yearly values of A_{1j} graphically. One can see that if the social discount rate is 7.5 percent, the average yearly cost per student through year 13 of the project (1978) will be about $23. In other words, when the estimate of total ITV expenditures through 1978 was divided by

---

[8] Comparing total average costs with those incurred by the Salvadorean government, it is interesting to note that government costs are totally insensitive to the social discount rate. This results from a somewhat coincidental balancing of two factors: on the one hand, increasing the social discount rate increases capital costs; but on the other, it increases the value of foreign loans.

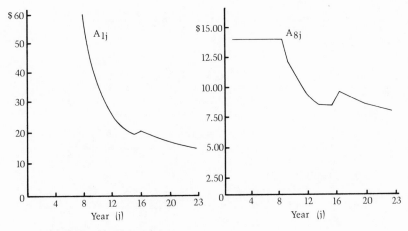

7.1. Yearly values for A_{1j} and A_{8j}

that of total student usage (each properly discounted), the result was $23. When the time horizon is extended to year 23 (1988), the result is approximately $15. The rise in the curve near year 16 (1981) reflects the need to replace production and transmission equipment.

Figure 7.1 also presents costs from the perspective of 1973 (that is, A_{8j}) rather than from the beginning of the project. In this case the j values less than 8 are constant, as indicated by the flat part of the curve. Viewed from 1973, the average costs through 1978 ($A_{8,13}$) were estimated at $8.50, as compared to the $23 predicted from ($A_{1,13}$). The small jump at year 16 is greatly magnified in the 1973 graph, since the fixed replacement costs account for a larger fraction of average costs from the perspective of 1973, and since they are discounted less, being much nearer in time.

Table 7.3 presents more exact computations of the average total costs of ITV, using the same costs and discounting as Figure 7.1 but taking various years as i and j values. The top row of the table corresponds to the A_{1j} graph in Figure 7.1 and the fifth row to the A_{8j} graph. Table 7.4 presents the same computations for Salvadorean government costs alone. Except in the lower-right corner, where the entries incorporate the bulk of the foreign loan repayments, costs here are lower than the total costs in Table 7.3. In the final analysis, the most appropriate estimate to use depends on one's temporal vantage point. In 1966, at the time of El Salvador's initial decision to

TABLE 7.3

Average Total Cost per Student from Year i to Year j for Third Cycle Schools

(1972 U.S. dollars)

Year i	Year j									
	1970	1972	1974	1976	1978	1980	1982	1984	1986	1988
1966	$254.95	$82.72	$44.49	$29.84	$23.11	$20.01	$18.88	$17.14	$15.95	$14.97
1969	134.63	60.50	34.24	23.71	18.73	16.53	15.96	14.59	13.67	12.89
1971		43.71	24.90	17.75	14.35	13.02	13.00	11.99	11.33	10.75
1972		17.92	13.55	10.95	9.45	9.15	9.80	9.18	8.80	8.44
1973			11.78	9.69	8.46	8.37	9.21	8.64	8.31	7.98
1974			9.75	8.52	7.58	7.73	8.77	8.23	7.92	7.61
1975				8.00	7.12	7.43	8.66	8.08	7.77	7.45
1976				6.95	6.48	7.09	8.58	7.95	7.63	7.30
1977					6.23	7.13	8.90	8.11	7.72	7.34
1978					6.51	7.55	9.57	8.47	7.96	7.50
1980						7.89	11.17	8.98	8.15	7.53
1984								5.21	5.58	5.32
1988										4.74

TABLE 7.4
Average Government Cost per Student from Year i to Year j for Third Cycle Schools
(1972 U.S. dollars)

Year i	1970	1972	1974	1976	1978	1980	1982	1984	1986	1988
1966	$177.52	$44.19	$25.37	$18.39	$14.93	$13.56	$13.52	$12.51	$11.84	$11.25
1969	70.79	24.48	16.28	12.96	11.04	10.47	10.92	10.25	9.81	9.40
1971		13.99	11.20	9.85	8.78	8.68	9.43	8.94	8.63	8.33
1972		11.25	9.84	8.98	8.10	8.15	9.03	8.57	8.29	8.01
1973			9.26	8.56	7.74	7.87	8.87	8.40	8.13	7.85
1974			9.75	8.52	7.58	7.78	8.89	8.38	8.09	7.80
1975				8.00	7.12	7.49	8.79	8.25	7.96	7.65
1976				6.95	6.48	7.16	8.73	8.14	7.84	7.52
1977					6.23	7.22	9.07	8.32	7.95	7.58
1978					6.51	7.68	9.78	8.72	8.22	7.77
1980						8.27	11.55	9.33	8.51	7.88
1984								5.56	5.92	5.64
1988										5.05

invest in ITV, the long-run average cost to the government through 1988 as given in Table 7.4 was the most useful number for El Salvador to consider. But by 1973 the value $A_{8,23}$ was perhaps the most useful for long-range planning. For short-term expansion or contraction decisions, the immediate marginal cost per student might be appropriate. If El Salvador had not received grants and loans, the total costs in Table 7.3 would be best.

For other countries wishing to learn from El Salvador's experience, the most useful estimate is perhaps the long term average cost as viewed from the first year of the ITV system ($A_{1,23}$ in Table 7.3). Assuming the 7.5-percent social discount, this was calculated at $14.97 in El Salvador; and if Salvadorean students were to view an average of 170 ITV hours per year, the cost per student-hour would be $0.09. It should be remembered that these figures assume an ITV system operating through 1988—and, more important, that they also depend on the rapid expansion of enrollment projected in Table 7.1.

FACTORS OFFSETTING THE COST OF ITV

The cost of ITV was necessarily a sizeable expenditure above whatever else was provided students in the classroom. However, ITV costs were partially offset by a reduction of other costs.

The principal cost of conventional classroom instruction is teachers' time, and the most immediate benefit of ITV in El Salvador was a reduction in teaching time per student. The amount of time expended per student depends on average class size, S, as well as on the relative length of students' and teachers' school weeks. If h_s is the number of hours a full-time student is in school each week, and h_t the number of hours per week put in by a full-time teacher, the student/teacher ratio, R, can be defined as $(h_t/h_s)S$. Thus, if teachers work two full shifts $(h_t/h_s = 2)$, the ratio for an average class size of 40 will be 80. The costs of teaching can be reduced by increasing S or h_t, or by decreasing h_s. If the offsetting mechanism is to be an increase in h_t, of course, teachers' salary increments must be kept proportionately lower.

In El Salvador, the Reform reduced costs by increasing both teaching hours and class size. Counterbalancing these savings were the costs of providing ITV (which was considered necessary to maintain the quality of schooling, given the other changes). It was possible to estimate what instructional expenditures per student would have been without ITV (E), as well as what they actually were after the introduction of ITV (E_{ITV}).[9] Our data were somewhat shaky and inconsistent, but these estimates are probably accurate to within 15 percent.

When the Reform instituted major scheduling changes in 1971, students were required to attend 25 hours of classes each week; similarly, the standard full-time teaching load was set at 25 classroom hours. At this time, before the great expansion in Third Cycle enrollment, the average class size was no more than 35. Using these figures, the student/teacher ratio, R, was 35. With an average teacher's salary of $1,800 per year for a 25-hour workweek, the total instructional expenditure per student would have been $52 per year in 1972, provided that the Reform had been mounted without ITV and that traditional class size had been maintained.[10]

However, ITV was introduced along with two other changes that affected costs per student. As the smaller Third Cycle schools were closed and more students matriculated at the larger ones, average class size increased dramatically. At the same time, most Third Cycle teachers were asked to increase their weekly teaching loads by 40 percent (from 25 to 35 hours), although their salaries were increased by only 20 percent (to $2,165). It is reasonable to assume that these changes would not have been possible without ITV. In fact, the Ministry planners wrote that one of the strongest reasons for extending ITV was "to help the teacher who sees himself as overburdened by double sessions."[11]

In the event, then, the teaching cost per student equaled the new wage, $2,165, divided by the new R value of $1.4S$, giving a figure of $1,546/S$, where S was the average class size following the introduction of ITV. This teaching cost, E, was added to the annualized ITV

[9] We use the term "instructional expenditures" to denote the costs of teacher retraining and television costs. This excludes costs for school administration, classroom space, and student supplies, all of which are assumed to be the same with or without ITV.

[10] See ODEPOR, *Plan Quinquenal del ramo educación* (San Salvador, 1972), p. 33.

[11] *Ibid.*

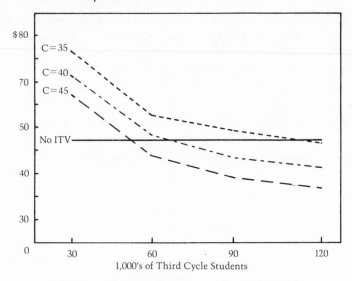

7.2. Instructional costs per student per year: with ITV in classes (C) of 35, 40, and 45 students; and in all classes without ITV

costs per student calculated earlier to give the annual per-student cost with ITV: $E_{ITV} = \$1{,}546/S + \$799{,}000/N + 1.10$.

It was not clear during the early years of the Reform what the average Third Cycle class size would eventually be. Therefore, in order to illustrate how S and N would jointly affect costs per student, Figure 7.2 was constructed to show how E_{ITV} varied with N for S values of 35, 40, and 45. The figure also graphs the assumed $52 value of E, which does not vary with N. All points on the E_{ITV} curves that lie below the E line are combinations of class size and total enrollment that have lower instructional costs per student with ITV than without it. For example, when $S = 40$, the cost per student per year will be less with ITV system than in the traditional system, provided that more than 60,000 students use ITV, and that the non-ITV classes retain the old class size and number of teaching hours. Under such assumptions, it was clear that the use of ITV in El Salvador's Reform was accompanied by a reduction in unit cost.[12]

[12] These estimates are based on Salvadorean government costs only. E and E_{ITV} crossover points would be at higher N levels if total costs were used for

SUMMARY AND IMPLICATIONS

The costs of El Salvador's ITV system were divided into two components: fixed costs (studio facilities, production costs, etc.), which are the same whatever the number of students watching; and variable costs (television receivers, student workbooks, etc.), which increase with the number of students in the audience. The total fixed costs per year (apportioning the capital cost over 25 years of the project under assumptions specified in the text) were estimated at $1.1 million, of which some $800,000 would eventually be paid by the Salvadorean government. The remainder was provided by grants from other countries, chiefly the United States. The variable cost (or additional cost per student) was about $1.10. In 1972 when 48,000 students were enrolled, the amount paid per student by the government of El Salvador alone was $17.75, and the total expenditure was $24.35. In a hypothetical year in which 96,000 students were enrolled, the total cost per student would be $12.73, and the cost to the Salvadorean government $9.42. Knowing the number of students actually enrolled in the first seven years of the project, and projecting enrollments through year 23 of the project, we could estimate the average cost per student during any part of that period. Over the full 23 years, this figure was estimated at about $14.

The introduction of ITV in El Salvador was accompanied by a sharp increase in class sizes and teaching loads (40 percent more classroom hours), with only a 20-percent increase in teachers' pay. These changes tended to offset the add-on costs of ITV. In 1973, when an estimated 60,000 students were using ITV, the cost per student ($47) was lower than the $52 per student that would have been expended had ITV not been used, class size not increased, and teaching load not changed. As enrollments increase, the cost per student of the ITV system continues to decrease, whereas the non-ITV cost per student does not change.

El Salvador's decision-makers had three somewhat contradictory objectives in planning their Educational Reform: they wished to

these estimates. Thus for $S = 35$, 40, and 45 crossover points would be at 166,000, 91,000 and 67,500, respectively. However, we believe that government costs and not total costs were the appropriate ones for these estimates, since those are the relevant costs for decision-makers.

expand enrollments at the postprimary level; they wished to hold down budget increases and, if possible, to decrease costs per student; and they wished to improve the quality of education. If only the first two objectives were to be met—expanded enrollment with a minimum increase in budget—ITV and the Reform were unnecessary. These objectives could have been attained simply by adopting policies that would stimulate enrollment (free tuition and automatic promotion) and lower the cost per student (increased class sizes and teaching loads). However, overburdened teachers and crowded facilities would not have been able to maintain learning quality, much less improve it. Expansion without ITV and its accompanying reforms would probably have led to greater dissatisfaction among teachers and to a considerable decline in learning as more students from disadvantaged backgrounds entered the system.

ITV, introduced in the context of the Reform, did satisfy the objective of maintaining quality. The evidence for this has been presented in previous chapters. And our findings indicate that quality was maintained without limiting enrollment or incurring unacceptable costs per student. A potential threat to instructional quality was certainly created by increasing class size and raising the student/teacher ratio; but this was offset by introducing ITV and the Reform. In fact, when enough students were enrolled, the saving per student of increasing the student/teacher ratio was greater than the add-on cost of ITV.

One may wonder whether some other instructional reform, coupled with an increase in the student/teacher ratio, could have been as effective as ITV but less expensive. Had the Salvadorean government not decided on ITV, a 50-percent increase in that ratio would have allowed for substantial investments in other areas without increasing costs per student. The evidence about learning patterns gained from our surveys, however, suggests that the Reform without ITV would not have been sufficient to maintain learning quality. Since no information could be gathered on alternative instructional systems, we cannot say whether an investment in some technology other than television, or in such things as additional teacher retraining, higher salaries, and better classroom resources would have been as effective as ITV.

CHAPTER EIGHT

Some Concluding Remarks

By the end of 1972, four years after El Salvador's Educational Reform began, approximately 10,000 students had completed grades 7 through 9 with television. This year also marked the completion of the first phase of ITV's development and the end of the initial five-year educational plan (1968-72). With the inauguration of a new production center and two additional transmitters outside the capital, the Ministry of Education had been able to expand the ITV system to virtually all students enrolled in grades 7-9 of El Salvador's public schools. The majority of private-school students at the Third Cycle level were also receiving televised instruction.

Thus El Salvador's Educational Reform, and particularly the ITV system, had accomplished most of what was hoped for under the original five-year timetable. The bottleneck to secondary education had been widened, and with each passing year more students poured into the seventh grade. An increasing percentage of these were disadvantaged rural students, who, owing to liberalized evaluation and promotion procedures, could now expect to complete the ninth grade. Largely because of ITV, the great expansion in enrollment did not precipitate a decline in learning. In fact, just the opposite occurred; students learned more under the Reform with ITV than they had under the traditional system.

Although ITV unquestionably constituted a major investment for El Salvador the Ministry of Education managed to offset some of its cost by increasing both classroom teachers' hours and class size. Given the projected rise in enrollments, the per-student costs of instruction under the Reform with ITV should eventually be lower than if the Reform had been introduced with traditional class size and teaching loads.

More students, superior learning, and a high probability of equal or lower costs per student: these are notable and impressive results. On the basis of the studies reported in this book, what general conclusions can now be drawn from El Salvador's use of television for educational reform, and how applicable are these conclusions to other countries? To begin with, it is useful to review ITV's performance from the perspective of both the individual classroom and the educational system as a whole.

ITV IN THE CLASSROOM

At the local level, ITV in El Salvador helped upgrade the quality of classroom instruction by providing the bulk of new curriculum content in five basic subjects on a week-to-week basis. The resulting standardization of lessons and teaching schedules was a key factor in the success of the Educational Reform. Unlike previous educational innovations, television was capable of reaching all parts of the school system simultaneously. This meant that classroom instruction could proceed at approximately the same rate throughout the country—something that was impossible in the traditional system, where rates of instruction varied greatly according to the experience, ability, and motivation of the classroom teachers. This equalizing aspect of ITV was further illustrated by the fact that television was the first educational resource ever to have been distributed more or less evenly in El Salvador. Formerly, urban schools had received far more attention and investment than had rural schools.

Of course, the fact that televised instruction was available throughout El Salvador and reached all classrooms simultaneously did not guarantee that the programs would be used properly, or that satisfactory learning would automatically result. The task of incorporating televised instruction into the school routine rested with the classroom teachers; but as the teachers themselves discovered, televised instruction greatly facilitated the introduction of new curricula and the maintenance of a steady rate of instruction.

In the final analysis, the Salvadorean policy of centralizing and standardizing classroom instruction through television had both positive and negative repercussions at the local level. ITV effectively shattered the rather static environment of the traditional classroom, in which the teacher's authority was unchallenged and in which instruction rarely consisted of anything but dictation by the teacher and passive note-taking and memorization by the students. Before the Reform, the typical Salvadorean secondary classroom was a dreary, regimented place, and not at all the friendly, "humanized" learning environment imagined by some of the Reform's critics both inside and outside the country.

Television disrupted the authoritarian pattern of the traditional Salvadorean secondary school by introducing new stimuli that students and teachers could not ignore. Naturally, some classrooms adjusted to the changed circumstances more creatively than others. In some classes, the televised lessons were only brief interludes in a continuing ritual of lectures and student recitation. In others, new patterns of interaction emerged as students and teachers responded enthusiastically to the new information and experiences delivered from the outside. An acceptance of television and the adoption of teaching methods that guaranteed the proper utilization of the medium effectively transformed the traditional patterns of student-teacher interaction. Over time, the majority of El Salvador's classroom teachers relinquished their monopoly of instruction and actually became quite comfortable in a team-teaching relationship with television.

Although their opinions differed widely, over time as well as by subject, most Salvadorean teachers believed that ITV provided a useful service by exposing their students to a range of learning that was simply unavailable at the local level. Indirectly, this judgment substantiated the role of the television teachers as "master teachers," individuals extremely well qualified in their subject specialties who were able to draw on a wealth of materials to convey any new concept.

In the view of many critics both inside and outside the country, most lessons produced in El Salvador still did not adequately exploit the creative potential of television. This criticism persisted in spite of test data suggesting that the overall quality of learning under the Reform was superior to that of the traditional system. The lack of stimulating, imaginative programming most likely accounts for a gradual decline observed in ITV's popularity among students and teachers in the third and fourth years of the Reform. Had more time and effort been devoted to the creative use of the medium and to the development of alternatives to the "talking head" style of television teaching, it is unlikely that audience enthusiasm would have waned. In televised English lessons, where creative techniques were emphasized, the series maintained a consistently high popularity throughout the Reform's early years. The acclaim given the English series was especially gratifying to its producers because the subject was traditionally among the least popular and most poorly taught in Salvadorean schools.

We do not wish to overemphasize the gradual decline in ITV's popularity, for to do so risks obscuring the system's significant impact on the quality of education in El Salvador. Despite a slippage in program "ratings," learning results continued to favor students who received televised instruction over those who received all elements of the Reform except television. Moreover, as students progressed from the seventh through the ninth grade, their hopes for more education and more prestigious careers continued to climb. This trend suggested that ITV and the other reforms were having positive effects on student motivation. At the same time, it may be argued, ITV and the other innovations could have been generating hopes and expectations that could not possibly be fulfilled and that actually ran counter to the economic-development arguments first put forward in support of the country's Educational Reform.

ITV IN THE EDUCATIONAL SYSTEM

The Salvadorean experience underscores the argument that ITV or any other instructional technology must be conceived in terms of broad system needs and objectives. ITV was not simply imposed over traditional practices and structures in El Salvador; rather, it was coordinated with other major changes in the country's school system. Accompanied by these other innovations, ITV was never considered to be a panacea by the government planners—a notion that has accompanied the development of ITV projects in other parts of the world.

Nevertheless, ITV did play a prime catalytic role in the Salvadorean Educational Reform because it dramatically called attention to the need for change in so many areas. When the government decided to invest in television, it was logical to revise the curriculum so that the broadcast lessons would carry the most modern knowledge and teaching methods. Similarly, when El Salvador introduced ITV in the classroom, it became apparent that something had to be done to prepare the classroom teacher for it; consequently, a major retraining program was organized. And so it went with reforms in supervision and evaluation, and with the provision of new materials for both teachers and students. Not all of these changes were successfully integrated; but major changes seldom come easily in any national bureaucracy.

A crucial factor in the development of El Salvador's ITV system was the support it received from the highest levels of government. Fidel Sanchez Hernández made the Educational Reform the major program of his presidency; and since Salvadorean presidents are constitutionally limited to a single five-year term, the ITV system had to be designed and implemented quickly in order to gain political visibility and approval. The demanding task of implementing Sanchez Hernández's mandate was entrusted to Walter Béneke. As chairman of the Educational Television Commission, and later as Minister of Education, Béneke was relentless in his commitment to upgrade all aspects of El Salvador's school system. Using television as the pacesetter for a wide range of changes, the Minister was personally involved in the day-to-day progress of each one of his reforms. Whether the Educational Reform in El Salvador would have succeeded without Béneke cannot, of course, be determined; but it is doubtful that so many simultaneous changes would have come about without so forceful a leader.

The importance of strong leadership and high-level support, however, calls attention to the general problem of institutionalizing change in organizations as resistant to innovation as a national school system or ministry of education. In fact, the institutionalization of ITV and the other reforms may even have been slowed somewhat by the very force of Béneke's leadership. By entering directly into many of the day-to-day decisions and problems of his various divisions, Béneke continually challenged his chief subordinates. This tendency impeded initiative and the development of problem-solving ability at lower administrative levels. It also retarded communication and cooperation between division leaders. Again, however, one cannot say whether these problems, which were deeply rooted in the bureaucracy of El Salvador's Ministry of Education, would have been any less troublesome had some other person been minister.

Béneke's uncompromising pursuit of the Reform's objectives also offended classroom teachers, who felt that many of the new programs were being implemented at their expense. The nationwide teachers' strikes of 1968 and 1971 illustrate the resistance that occurred at the local level when teachers and school administrators were required to implement programs they had not helped formulate. Naturally, some changes were integrated into the school system more easily than others. ITV and the new Third Cycle curricula were accepted without great trouble. New evaluation and promotion policies were also accepted, though not integrated so fully. But the closing of numerous teacher training schools was resented at first, even though the consequent drop in teachers' unemployment and the high praise later accorded the centralized teacher retraining program eventually helped win teachers' approval.

The transformation of school supervisors from supervisor-inspector to supervisor-counselor presented the greatest single difficulty. This new role was a very unfamiliar one in El Salvador, and the supervisors initially opposed it as leading to a loss of authority and prestige. Ministry of Education bureaucrats also opposed it, since they initially had no control over it.

The lesson here is that no matter how great or obvious the need, educational innovations cannot be viewed outside a country's political context. Before so complex an innovation as classroom television can be introduced, careful attention must be paid to the administrative and institutional variables that will affect its rate of acceptance in the school system.

The Salvadorean experience clearly shows the advantages of putting local people in charge of developing all aspects of a new ITV system rather than relying on outside advisers. El Salvador did receive substantial foreign assistance in the early years; but after four years, an experienced Salvadorean staff was firmly established, and the outlook for continuing and expanding the ITV system was better than in other countries that had relied more heavily on foreign experts to do the actual production and teleteaching. This quick changeover had some drawbacks. As we have seen, for example, one of the classroom teachers' most persistent complaints was the uneven quality of the television lessons. It would seem that if a country wants to "learn by doing" (which has advantages over the long term), it must allow enough time before going on the air to train production teams, to let them gain experience, and to test and remake as many programs as possible.

Our observations also suggest that beginning ITV one grade at a time avoids many problems that may occur when the medium is introduced in a number of grades simultaneously. In El Salvador, it was possible to try out television for a year in 32 pilot seventh-grade classrooms before expanding it to the entire school system. And during the first three years of broadcasting the producers were able to revise and improve the vast majority of Third Cycle programs before they were transmitted on a nationwide basis.

One peculiar advantage El Salvador had in expanding its ITV system to the entire country was its small size. This has implications for other countries at two levels: physical distance and bureaucratic complexity. Most towns in El Salvador are within a few hours of the capital. Moreover, the size of the educational establishment was such that Béneke could bring about significant changes through his vigorous actions. Larger countries may find more difficulty in changing because of the sheer size of their educational establishments.

ITV systems never develop quite as smoothly or as quickly as expected, and El Salvador's was no exception. One of the more obvious reasons why the project fell behind schedule was the 1969 war with Honduras, which led to the freezing of foreign-aid funds and delayed the approval of a major loan from the United States. Moreover, El Salvador, like other countries, discovered that it took more time than expected to build up the administrative apparatus needed to design and coordinate such a large number of reforms. Still, by virtue of its local origins, its reform context, its strong leadership, and its proven ability to overcome difficult administrative problems, the ITV system's continuation and expansion seems more promising in El Salvador than in other countries that have launched television projects in the last fifteen years.

The appropriateness of the Salvadorean model for other countries depends ultimately on those nations' own estimates of ITV's potential usefulness, and on the importance they place on formal education within their overall development strategy. No matter how well planned and executed an educational reform may be, if it does not respond effectively to a society's real economic and social needs, the benefits to that society will be marginal. In evaluating El Salvador's accomplishments, one must ask if the social and economic benefits the country envisioned were realistic, and whether they are the same returns other nations might desire.

In their original planning documents, Salvadorean planners emphasized their country's need for more middle-level technical manpower, and through the Educational Reform they hoped to prepare young people for technical jobs in industry and agriculture. But by 1972 there were still relatively few technical jobs for Third Cycle graduates, who in any case were inclined to stay in school rather than enter the job market. If the country's high unemployment rate continues, and if there is no economic expansion to match the large increase in school enrollments, students will be forced to reconsider the kinds of middle-level jobs they currently refuse as unsuitable. As the demand for employment increases, the jobs themselves may also be reevaluated in terms of the academic credentials necessary to hold them; and over time all but the lowest positions may require a ninth-grade education.

Though conceding that employment is indeed likely to be a problem for Third Cycle graduates in the immediate future, Salvadorean planners believe that in the long run their economy will meet the challenge. By investing so heavily in secondary education, they feel, El Salvador will create a labor pool of adequate size and quality to attract investment, which in turn will generate new technical jobs. This expectation may or may not be fulfilled. In any case, planners from other countries must question whether such hopes are adequate justification for investing heavily in ITV and educational reform.

Of course, the rationale for mounting a comprehensive educational reform in El Salvador was not limited to the argument that it would help provide more jobs. The government planners also had strong political and philosophical justifications. Above all, they believed that nine years of basic education should be the right of every Salvadorean child, regardless of the costs of such a policy to the society as a whole. In spite of these democratic ideals, however, the social impact of ITV was still relatively small in 1972, considering the large number of children and adults who had no contact with the school system. The opportunities were there, but not yet fully exploited.

The introduction of ITV and the other reforms may, in the long run, reduce costs per student; but the consequent increases in enrollment will require massive investment of scarce resources for years to come. In 1972, the Ministry of Education consumed some 36 percent of the national budget. Such a concentration of resources reflects a tremendous confidence that the younger generation of Salvadoreans will eventually solve their country's pressing economic and social problems—and, at least tacitly, a lack of faith in older generations to do so. In Minister Béneke's words: "I do not wish to give solutions now, nor pretend to solve the next decade's problems. I am ... preparing a new consciousness among the young, and the product of that new consciousness should be of a high order. I cannot with my present mentality give solutions. . . . They [the young] will produce the solutions!"[1]

Other countries, burdened by their own economic problems and pressures for social change, and wishing to learn from El Salvador's successful application of ITV, may not share Béneke's bias or be willing to allocate their educational resources exclusively to school-aged youth. And indeed, in drafting the second five-year educational plan (1973-77),[2] Salvadorean planners turned their attention for the first time to the needs of other groups, such as primary schoolteachers and the adult population at large. In so doing, they acknowledged that schooling alone would never solve deeply rooted economic problems, and that modern technology is no substitute for basic political and social reform. With that proviso, however, the Salvadorean experience does point to a promising role for the mass media in the resolution of the Third World's pressing educational problems.

[1] Walter Béneke, as quoted in Cornell Capa and J. Mayone Stycos, *Margin of life* (New York: Grossman, 1974), p. 186.

[2] The draft plan, not yet entirely implemented, is set forth in ODEPOR, *Plan Quinquenal del ramo educación 1973-77.* San Salvador, June 1972.

Appendixes

Chronology of ITV and the Reform

1960 The possibility of introducing ITV is discussed in El Salvador's newspapers.

1962 A survey by Japan Broadcasting Corporation engineers is arranged by Walter Béneke, Salvadorean Ambassador to Japan. The survey team recommends a national ITV system.

1963 President Julio Rivera establishes an Educational Television Commission to recommend a national plan for ITV by 1964, but progress drags. Some young Salvadoreans are sent to Japan for a year of engineering training, but there are no ITV jobs when they return.

1964 The Department of Educational Television is created within the Ministry of Education; for two years it has no leader and no budget.

1965 Béneke returns from Japan, and is appointed chairman of the Educational Television Commission (ETC). New appointments are made, and the Commission begins to hold weekly meetings. The Commission studies the experiences of other countries with ITV and conducts a statistical analysis of the Salvadorean educational system.

1966 The ETC decides that ITV should be introduced first in grades 7-9, the Third Cycle, and recommends that it be administered by an autonomous institution reporting directly to the President, rather than by a new bureau within the Ministry of Education.

1967 The production of experimental programs is begun, using facilities rented from a commercial TV station.

In April President Fidel Sanchez Hernández hears Lyndon B. Johnson speak at Punta del Este of the possibility of financing a pilot ITV project somewhere in Latin America; he puts El Salvador's case before U.S. officials. An AID survey team recruited by the National Association of Educational Broadcasters recommends a favorable response to the proposal, but pushes for a large project aimed at the primary grades. Salvadoreans object to this and eventually prevail.

Béneke is named Minister of Education in July, and opposition to placing ITV under the Ministry evaporates.

The Salvadorean government submits its formal proposal to USAID.

1968 The project agreement is signed. USAID agrees to contribute $653,000 to the start-up costs of ITV—largely for studio and transmission equipment, graphic arts equipment, printing machinery, and 100 television receivers.

A U.S. loan of $1.9 million is negotiated to back up the AID contribution and make it possible for El Salvador to construct new studio and transmission facilities, and to provide receivers to cover most of the country.

Minister Béneke closes most of the normal schools, which had been overproducing primary teachers, and establishes a new, centralized normal school at the San Andrés campus.

In September a temporary studio is equipped at San Andrés.

The first 20 members of the ITV staff begin on-the-job training.

USAID sends in its first group of advisers in production, graphics, film, curriculum revision, printing, utilization, and evaluation.

A tentative revision of the seventh-grade curriculum is completed in November and given to the ITV production teams and instructors at San Andrés. The production teams are given three months to prepare classroom materials, teacher's guides, and the first TV programs. The normal school faculty also have three months in which to retrain 100 teachers for the pilot ITV classrooms and prepare 12 candidates for positions as utilization supervisors.

1969 The new curriculum and ITV are introduced in 32 seventh-grade classes when school opens in February.

A nine-month retraining program begins for 250 Third Cycle teachers.

War breaks out between El Salvador and Honduras in July. USAID funds to both countries are frozen.

1970 The AID freeze on funds to El Salvador is lifted.

In February the Reform curriculum is introduced in all seventh-grade classes, with ITV in 219 of 400 classrooms.

The 32 pilot classes begin eighth grade with the new curriculum and ITV programs.

A second group of 250 Third Cycle teachers begins the nine-month retraining program.

The Salvadorean National Assembly gives final authorization in October for an AID loan to finance new studio and transmission facilities.

1971 The Ministry of Education is reorganized. The Third Cycle is revamped and renamed Third Cycle of Basic Education.

The system of "oriented promotion" is introduced, under which almost all students will pass each year. Testing and evaluation are modernized.

Tuition is eliminated for the Third Cycle, opening up the seventh grade to all qualified graduates of the Second Cycle. This results in overcrowded classrooms and heavy teaching loads.

The new curriculum and ITV are extended as widely as possible in grades 7 and 8.

The 32 pilot classes begin using ITV in ninth grade.

Retraining begins for a third group of 250 Third Cycle teachers.

A new curriculum is introduced in grades 1-6. Primary teachers receive a one-week crash retraining program via ITV. Retraining continues via ITV on Saturday mornings.

A six-month retraining program for school directors begins.

Salvadorean teachers strike in July, asking higher pay and a reduction in workloads. Most schools greatly disorganized. ITV broadcasts previously taped lessons to the seventh- and eighth-grade classes, that remain in session. Ninth-grade ITV goes off the air for the remainder of the year.

Teachers' strike settled in September, but many schools still disorganized by teacher transfers.

Béneke resigns as Minister of Education and is named Minister of Foreign Affairs. Antonia Portillo de Galindo is appointed Minister of Education.

1972 ITV programs revised to reflect the new curriculum and new printed materials.

New studios at Santa Tecla open in February.

Reform programs and ITV extended throughout Third Cycle.

Another 230 Third Cycle teachers begin retraining.

New Minister of Education, Rogelio Sanchez, appointed in July as a new government takes office.

New Five-Year Plan provides for introduction of ITV in Second Cycle; ITV also to be used extensively in adult education and retraining teachers.

ITV personnel receive extensive retraining in the use of behavioral objectives, formative evaluation, and the qualitative aspects of improving programming—under the auspices of the Stanford research team and Ministry officials.

1973 New government TV channels and production studio officially inaugurated.

The Basic Skills Tests and Learning Analyses

The general ability and reading tests used in our evaluation were part of the Inter-American Series published by Guidance Testing Associates of Austin, Texas (Spanish versions validated in Puerto Rico). Level 3 tests were administered to Cohort A in seventh grade in 1969; at all other times Level 4 exams were used.

Table B.1 details the subsections of the tests, the number of questions in each, and the reliability of the results. The reliabilities given are those of the tests administered in the eighth grade to the 900 students of Cohort A and the 700 students of Cohort B, calculated according to the following formula (see D. Heise, "Separating reliability and stability in test-retest correlation," *Amer. Soc. Rev.*, 34: 93-101):

$$r_{22} = \frac{r_{12} \times r_{23}}{r_{13}}$$

Here r_{22} is the reliability of the second exam and the other terms are correlations between exams—r_{13} is that of the first and third, etc.

The reliabilities indicate that the tests used were adequate for El Salvador, at least on the surface. With the exception of the low numerical ability figures for both cohorts, and the low reliability for speed of comprehension in Cohort A, these reliabilities were close to those reported by Guidance Testing for a parallel-form administration with small Puerto Rican samples.

The contributions of the several components of each test to the total test mean were remarkably stable over time and across cohorts. As the total test mean increased for a cohort, so did each of the subtest means (Table B.2). Gains were not weighted toward verbal ability and away from numerical ability, for example. Also, despite changes in the socioeconomic makeup of succeeding cohorts, the contributions of the subtests varied minimally.

GENERAL ABILITY LEARNING MODELS

The conclusions stated in Chapter 3 concerning general ability learning and the interaction effects related to ITV and background variables were

TABLE B.I
The General Ability and Reading Tests

Test and subsection	No. of items	Reliability	
		Cohort A	Cohort B
General ability	150	.87	.80
Verbal		.82	.75
Sentence completion	25		
Word relations	25		
Nonverbal		.80	.87
Analogies	24		
Classification	26		
Numerical		.59	.67
Computation	26		
Number series	24		
Reading	125	.79	.77
Vocabulary	45	.70	.83
Speed of comprehension	30	.48	.70
Level of comprehension	50	.64	.63

TABLE B.2
Subtest Means as Percentages of Total Test Means

Subtest	Cohort A		Cohort B		Cohort C	
	Mar. 1970	Oct. 1971	Mar. 1970	Oct. 1972	Mar. 1971	Oct. 1972
G.A. verbal	37%	37%	34%	37%	33%	36%
G.A. nonverbal	37	37	40	37	41	38
G.A. numerical	26	26	25	26	26	26
Rd. vocabulary	43	45	45	45	45	45
Rd. speed comp.	23	23	22	22	22	23
Rd. level compr.	34	33	33	33	33	32

the result of a fairly complex analysis. For those interested, the various aspects of this procedure are detailed here.

All schools in the capital, San Salvador, were eliminated from the analysis, since no cohort had matched ITV and non-ITV samples there. This decision limited the variance on the urbanization variable and may have obscured some actual urbanization effects.

Although the basic analysis procedures were applied to all three cohorts, there were differences in the measurement model for the general ability variable underlying each analysis; these resulted from variations in the number of general ability scores available for each cohort. Cohort A scores were available from four test administrations: beginnings of grades 7, 8, and 9, and end of grade 9. Cohort B was tested at three of these points, omitting the beginning of grade 9. And Cohort C students took the test only at the beginning of grade 7 and the end of grade 8. We shall trace the analysis of Cohort B data, occasionally noting points at which it differed from the other analyses.

Before estimating the effects of other variables on general ability initial scores and gain scores, we defined a measurement model for the general ability variable itself. This allowed us to estimate the error component of each general ability score, and hence to disattenuate the correlations of other variables with the general ability variables. This, in turn, lent greater precision to the regression coefficients reported below.

The measurement model chosen followed the work of Wiley and Wiley (1970, in *Amer. Soc. Rev.*, 35: 112-17). The model states:

$$GA1 = GA1_t + e_1$$
$$GA3 = mGA1_t + GA13_t + e_3$$
$$GA6 = n(mGA1_t + GA13_t) + GA36_t + e_6$$

$GA1$, $GA3$, and $GA6$ represent observed Cohort B general ability scores at the beginning of seventh, the beginning of eighth, and the end of ninth grade, respectively. $GA1_t$ is the true-score component of $GA1$; $GA13_t$ and $GA36_t$ are true-score components that represent new information first appearing at measurement wave 3 and measurement wave 6, respectively. The scaling parameters m and n reflect the influence of true-score components of a given exam on observed scores on a subsequent exam. The error components, e_1, e_3 and e_6 are assumed to have a mean of zero and to be uncorrelated both with one another and with the true score components.

Given three observed test scores, there are three variances ($V[GA1]$, $V[GA3]$, $V[GA6]$) and three covariances ($C[GA1, GA3]$, $C[GA1, GA6]$, and $C[GA3, GA6]$). But the measurement model as specified has eight parameters (three true-score variances, three error variances and two scaling parameters), and thus would be underidentified unless a constraint is introduced. Following Wiley and Wiley (1970), then, the three error variances were defined as equal, leaving the measurement model with only six unknown values (three true-score variances, two scaling parameters, and one value for error variance). The model proves to be exactly identified under this constraint.[1]

To specify the influence of background variables on general ability and reading skills as students entered grade 7, straightforward multiple regression equations were calculated for Cohorts A and B, using the general ability scores (corrected for unreliability) as dependent variables. The results are summarized in Table B.3.

[1] The Cohort A data, with four measurement waves, permitted a less constrained model. Rather than assuming that all four error variances were equal, it was only necessary to consider the first two equal and the last two equal; and even so the model was overidentified. Cohort C data, with only two measurement waves, did not permit the estimation of an explicit measurement model; and they were analyzed under the usual assumption of perfect reliability.

TABLE B.3

The Influence of Background Variables on General Ability and Reading

Variable and correlations	Gen. ability, by cohort			Reading, by cohort		
	A	B	C	A	B	C
Age						
Standardized	− .20	− .21	− .24	− .14	− .12	− .18
F ratio	25.3	27.2	27.6	12.3	7.9	15.4
Unstandardized	−2.48	−2.27	−2.31	−1.73	−1.00	−1.34
Sex						
Standardized	.13	.19	.19	.21	.16	.16
F ratio	11.9	22.4	18.0	31.1	17.4	13.3
Unstandardized	4.58	6.30	5.98	7.38	4.51	4.02
Father's educ.						
Standardized	− .02 ·	.06	.01	.03	.11	.03
F ratio	.18	1.7	.05	.35	4.9	.23
Unstandardized	− .26	.71	.16	.36	.99	.27
Mother's educ.						
Standardized	.03	.12	.03	− .01	.07	.03
F ratio	.35	6.5	.37	.06	2.1	.41
Unstandardized	.42	1.65	.50	− .17	.76	.42
Affluence						
Standardized	.09	.12	.00	.02	.15	.09
F ratio	4.4	8.4	.01	.35	12.8	3.04
Unstandardized	3.76	4.78	.12	1.1	4.77	2.48
Urbanization						
Standardized	− .11	− .12	− .18	− .09	− .21	− .25
F ratio	7.5	8.7	15.8	5.6	27.7	31.5
Unstandardized	−2.04	−1.91	−2.50	−1.80	−2.76	−2.76
N	670	575	452	663	520	452
r^2	.09	.20	.15	.08	.21	.17
Constant	128.93	85.46	87.86	91.18	51.47	56.05

NOTE: Reading equations were not corrected for unreliability; Cohort A and B general ability equations were corrected, and no correction was made for Cohort C general ability.

In Chapter 3 we presented data supporting the contention that ITV affected students' gains in general ability scores. These results can be restated in a regression format (Table B.4). The final general ability score for each cohort is the dependent variable. Predictors, entered simultaneously, include the initial general ability score, the six background variables, and a dichotomous variable representing learning condition (ITV = 1; no ITV = 0). In each case the coefficients for the instructional condition variable prove to be significant. By examining the unstandardized coefficients, one can see the number of extra points gained by the average student in an ITV class (controlling for initial general ability and background characteristics).

For Cohort B, the classrooms forming the control group of the attempted experiment (see pp. 57-59), which had all the elements of the Reform

*Influence of ITV and Background Variables on
Final General Ability Score*

Variables and sample conditions	Standardized, by cohort			Unstandardized, by cohort		
	A	B	C	A	B	C
Age	−.22	−.12	−.13	−2.85	−1.45	−1.59
F ratio	(68.6)	(45.5)	(13.0)			
Sex	.08	.03	.13	2.96	1.18	5.46
F ratio	(10.7)	(3.3)	(15.1)			
Father's educ.	−.04	.02	.02	−.57	.26	.27
F ratio	(1.8)	(1.0)	(.15)			
Mother's educ.	−.06	−.09	.02	−.97	−1.46	.29
F ratio	(4.08)	(22.3)	(.13)			
Affluence	−.07	−.07	−.01	−2.89	−3.35	−.51
F ratio	(5.7)	(17.9)	(.08)			
Urbanization	.04	−.01	−.06	.70	−.21	−1.05
F ratio	(1.9)	(.47)	(2.7)			
Initial general ability score	.70	.90	.58	.71	1.06	.73
F ratio	(731.1)	(2768.2)	(251.3)			
Instructional condition[a]	.10	.07	.06	4.18	2.74	2.54
F ratio	(17.3)	(17.4)	(2.58)			
N	670	575	452			
r^2	.60	.87	.49			
Constant				64.95	41.40	46.64

[a] ITV = 1; no ITV = 0.

except ITV, were combined with the rest of the matched sample of non-ITV schools to form the control sample for the analysis. Since instructional conditions in all these classrooms were similar (with the exception that some classes were in schools where other classes had ITV and some in schools entirely without ITV), this appeared to be justified.[2]

The final series of hypotheses under test suggested the existence of an interaction effect, by which the effect of given background variables on general ability gains would be different for ITV and non-ITV students. For example, was the advantage of boys over girls less among students who studied with television than among students who studied without it? Three steps were involved in these analyses.

1. First, we narrowed down the list of background variables to those that showed some evidence of significant interaction effects, using and extending

[2] For Cohort A, the experimental control classrooms could not be combined with the matched control sample, since this contained only traditional classrooms that used no elements of the Reform. As a result, the Cohort A experimental control classrooms were dropped from our analyses. Cohort C had only matched ITV and Reform-without-ITV samples.

the regression equations mentioned earlier. Variables representing the inter-action of each of the six background variables with ITV were created by multiplying the deviation score of the background variable by the instruc-tional condition variable. Then the partial correlation of each interaction variable with the final general ability score was calculated, after all the previously used predictor variables (the six background variables, instruc-tional condition, and initial general ability) had been entered into the regression equation. Interaction variables with significant ($p < .05$) partial correlations in two or more cohorts were selected for the next step; these included age, father's education, and urbanization.

2. For each of the three variables, a regression equation was estimated for the combined ITV/non-ITV sample, predicting the final general ability score from five of the six background variables and excluding the one variable whose interaction effects were being explored. Thus when age was the variable of interest for Cohort B, the following unstandardized equa-tion was generated:

$$GA_{6t} = -2.93 \text{ urban} + 7.9 \text{ sex} + 1.42 \text{ father's education} +$$
$$1.36 \text{ mother's education} + 3.91 \text{ affluence} + 77.11$$

3. The ITV and non-ITV subsamples were divided. A new variable, pre-dictors without age, was generated for each subsample using the equation in step 2. Then a four-variable correlation matrix (final general ability, initial general ability, age and Pr w/o age) was calculated (and disattenuated within each subsample for Cohorts A and B). From those matrices a re-gression equation was calculated for each instructional condition sub-sample, taking the form

$$GA_{6t} = b_1 \, GA_{1t} + b_2 \, Pr \text{ w/o age} + b_3 \text{ age} + a_1$$

For Cohort B, the two unstandardized equations were for ITV,

$$GA_{6t} = 1.03 \, GA1_t - .11 \, Pr \text{ w/o age} - 1.6 \text{ age} + 53.18$$

and for non-ITV,

$$GA_{6t} = 1.03 \, GA1_t + .05 \, Pr \text{ w/o age} - .71 \text{ age} + 25.45$$

The important comparison is that between coefficients of the age vari-able. ITV students lost 1.6 points for each year they were older in a given grade. Non-ITV students lost .7 points. This particular finding supports a gap-opening hypothesis concerning ITV: that younger students have a relatively greater advantage over older students in a given grade. Non-ITV students lost .7 points in Cohort B, but this particular finding was not replicable for other cohorts—in particular, Cohort A showed just the opposite result. In fact, we found that no background variable had a con-sistent interaction effect across all three cohorts. Complete results for the three variables are given in Tables B.5, B.6, and B.7.

TABLE B.5
Age/ITV Interaction

Sample group and correlation	Initial test	Pred. w/o age	Age	Const.	r^2	N
Cohort A (predicting GA6):						
ITV (B)	.69 (480)	1.31 (21)	−2.36 (34)	30.72	.58	450
β value	.69	.14	− .19			
Trad. (B)	.70 (211)	1.30 (12)	−4.24 (37)	61.45	.61	200
β value	.67	.16	− .29			
Cohort B:						
ITV (B)	1.03 (1,021)	−.11 (2.5)	−1.60 (23.3)	53.18	.78	360
β value	.86	−.04	− .13			
Control (B)	1.03 (583)	.05 (.2)	− .71 (4.0)	25.45	.79	215
β value	.854	.02	− .07			
Cohort C (predicting GA4):						
ITV (B)	.70 (166)	.38 (9.8)	−1.40 (7)	24.13	.46	340
β value	.58	.14	− .12			
Control (B)	.83 (77)	.43 (4.5)	−1.39 (3.3)	12.33	.54	130
β value	.62	.14	− .12			

NOTE: Cohorts A and B disattenuated; Cohort C attenuated. Numbers in parentheses are F ratios.

TABLE B.6
Father's Education/ITV Interaction

Sample group and correlation	Initial test	Pred. w/o father's education	Father's education	Const.	r^2	N
Cohort A:						
ITV (B)	.71 (503)	.89 (41.7)	− .53 (1.5)	3.31	.57	450
β value	.71	.20	− .04			
Trad. (B)	.72 (240)	1.52 (45)	.54 (.8)	−9.42	.62	200
β value	.69	.31	.04			
Cohort B:						
ITV (B)	1.01 (967)	.22 (12.3)	− .27 (.6)	5.76	.77	360
β value	.85	.10	− .02			
Control (B)	1.02 (596)	.22 (10.7)	− .88 (4.4)	3.32	.80	215
β value	.85	.12	− .07			
Cohort C:						
ITV (B)	.71 (169)	.39 (14)	.75 (1.2)	2.04	.46	340
β value	.58	.17	.05			
Control (B)	.80 (73.3)	.59 (11.8)	−2.60 (3.1)	−12.59	.56	130
β value	.60	.25	− .11			

NOTE: Cohorts A and B disattenuated; Cohort C attenuated. Numbers in parentheses are F ratios.

TABLE B.7
Urbanization/ITV Interaction

Sample group and correlation	Initial test	Pred. w/o urban.	Urban.	Const.	r^2	N
Cohort A (predicting GA6):						
ITV (B)	.70 (497)	.93 (45)	.49 (.5)	.16	.58	450
β value	.70	.21	.02			
Trad. (B)	.73 (215)	1.26 (33)	.90 (1.5)	−6.80	.60	200
β value	.69	.26	.06			
Cohort B (predicting GA6):						
ITV (B)	1.01 (996)	.27 (19.6)	.70 (2.5)	− .79	.78	360
β value	.84	.12	.04			
Trad. (B)	1.03 (610)	.07 (1.1)	−1.78(9.9)	18.76	.80	215
β value	.86	.04	− .10			
Cohort C (predicting GA4):						
ITV (B)	.70 (166)	.45 (18.6)	− .81 (1.1)	2.78	.46	340
β value	.58	.19	− .04			
Trad. (B)	.82 (75)	.45 (6)	−1.37 (1.5)	−4.35	.53	130
β value	.62	.17	− .08			

NOTE: Numbers in parentheses are F ratios.

Sample Research Instruments

*For space reasons the questionnaires and forms in this section
(translated from the Spanish originals) have been reproduced
two to a page, turned 90 degrees. The first page appears below.*

I. Sample Student Survey

Full Name: _____

Name of School: _____

Grade: _____   Section: _____

INSTRUCTIONS: THIS IS NOT A TEST. THERE ARE NO CORRECT OR
INCORRECT ANSWERS. WHAT COUNTS IS YOUR OWN
OPINION. PLEASE ANSWER WITH SINCERITY.

Each one of the following questions has one or more answers. Put an
"X" in the blank that corresponds to your answer. In those cases
for which you are asked to fill in information, do so in the appropriate space.

Section I

1. Age:

2. Sex:

3. Date of birth:

4. Write the total number of people who live in your house (including yourself and servants, if there are any):

5. Of the following people, which ones live in your house?

   mother
   father
   brothers and sisters
   grandparents
   other relatives
   others who are not relatives

6. What is your father's occupation?

7. What is your mother's occupation?

8. Indicate your parents' level of education:

	Father	Mother		Father	Mother
Didn't study			Commercial course		
Part of primary			High school		
All of primary			University		
Third Cycle					

9. How long does it take you to get to school every day?

Less than 15 minutes __   Between 15 and 30 minutes __
Between 30 minutes and an hour __   More than an hour __

Section II

10. Of the following information media, which do you have at home?

newspapers __   radio __   books __
magazines __   television __

11. Outside of school, how many times did you watch television last week?

never __   three or four times __   every day __
one or two times __   five or six times __

12. Approximately how long do you listen to the radio each day?

never __   three or four hours each day __
less than an hour each day __   more than four hours each day __
one or two hours each day __

13. How frequently did you read newspapers last week?

never __   1-2 times __   3-4 times __   5-6 times __   every day __

14. How frequently did you read magazines last week?

never __   1-2 times __   3-4 times __   more than 4 times __

15. How many books did you read last year?

none __   1-3 __   4-10 __

16. How frequently did you go to the movies last month?

never __   1-2 times __   3-4 times __   more than 4 times __

17. Where do you usually see commercial television?

in your house __   in the house of relatives __
in a friend's house __   in some other place __

18. What is your favorite commercial television program?

19. What day or days is that program on?

20. How often do you see each one of the following programs -- every week, once or twice a month, rarely, or never?

Tarzan   Oficina para todos
Tom Jones   Tierra de gigantes

Section III

INSTRUCTIONS:

In this section you will find a series of statements. There are five possible answers for each statement that go from "Completely agree" to "Completely disagree." You should choose the answer that most closely approximates your own opinion and put an "X" on the corresponding line. Example:

Playing with a ball is lots of fun.

Completely agree	Agree	Undecided	Disagree	Completely disagree

Please answer the following statements that are about educational television. Remember we want to know your personal opinions.

21. You learn more during classes with television than during classes without television.

22. Classes with television are more difficult.

23. One can see the teleclasses clearly.

24. It is easier to understand classes with television than classes without television.

25. Classes with television do not give one enough opportunity to express his opinions.

26. My parents know a lot about the use of television in my school.

27. Classroom teachers seem to prefer teaching with television.

28. It is more difficult to ask questions in classes with television than in other classes.

29. Classes with television are more enjoyable than classes without television.

30. From which of the following situations do you learn most? do you learn least?

    from your own study
    from your courses with classroom teachers
    from written work or group projects in class
    from Educational Television programs

Section IV

31. Which subject do you most like to study? Which least?

    Mathematics   Natural sciences
    Social studies   English
    Spanish   All of the above

32. How far do you intend to go in school?

    Finish Third Cycle
    Finish a career course, after Third Cycle
    Finish high school
    Finish the university
    Specialize after graduating from the university

33. How sure are you that you will finish the studies you hope to complete?

    I am certain I will not finish
    I believe I will not finish
    I may finish
    I believe I will finish
    I am certain I will finish

34. Of the following reasons, mark the most important one that you believe would not permit you to study as much as you want to:

    Studies will be too difficult
    Opposition of my parents
    Lack of money
    Lack of opportunity
    Other reasons
    No reason

35. What level of studies do you consider necessary for the majority of the Salvadorean population?

    Primary school   Carrera Corta   University
    Third Cycle   Bachillerato

36. Who is most concerned about your education?

    Father
    Mother
    Another relative
    Another person who is not a member of the family
    No one

37. Which career would you most like to follow when you finish your studies?

38. The career you mention was chosen by you for which of the following reasons?

    It pays a good salary
    It is a respected career
    That career is one that helps other people
    It is a "short" career
    You prefer it, but for no particular reason
    Other reasons

39. If for some reason you are unable to pursue the career you selected in Question 37, what kind of work will you probably do?

40. What career would your parents most like you to have?

41. How frequently do you talk to your parents about the careers you might have?

    Never   From time to time   Very frequently
    Frequently

42. When you finish your studies, with whom would you like to work?

    The government   A large company
    A small company   On my own
    With someone in my family

43. When you finish your studies and begin to work, where would you like to live?

    In a small town
    In a city other than San Salvador
    In San Salvador
    Outside the country

44. When you finish your studies, would you be willing to live and work in a small town?

   Completely willing   More or less willing
   More or less unwilling   Completely unwilling

45. What monthly salary do you believe is necessary to live decently?

   100-200 colones*   200-300 colones
   300-400 colones   400-500 colones
   500-600 colones   over 600 colones

46. Do you work in addition to attending school?

   Work for a salary outside of the home
   Work with parents or relatives and receive a salary
   Work only on household chores
   Do not work regularly

47. If at the end of Third Cycle you were to be offered a good paying job but one that would not permit you to continue your studies, would you take the job?

   Yes   No   Undecided

48. What kinds of things do you like to do most in your spare time? (Three favorites were listed.)

Section V

49. How will life be for the majority of students in your class?

   Very similar to that of their parents
   Almost like that of their parents
   Generally different from that of their parents
   Very different from that of their parents

50. What is the best way to get ahead in a job?

   To be intelligent
   To work hard
   To work a long time in the same place
   To know how to work well with other people
   To have friends or relatives who have influence

*1 colon equals $.40 U.S.

51. Consider each one of the following occupations and mark down whether you would be happy or unhappy to do that kind of work.

   Bookkeeper   Accountant
   Day-laborer   Architect
   Engineer   Electrician
   Small farmer   High school teacher
   Brick-layer   Nurse
   Doctor   Bilingual secretary
   Industrial technician Insurance agent
   Chauffeur   Primary school teacher
   Lawyer   Business manager
   Soldier

52. Getting a good education is worth the sacrifice of being away from one's family.

Completely agree	Agree	Undecided	Disagree	Completely disagree

53. In general, it is better to accept a good job when it is offered, rather than continue one's education with the hope of getting a better job in the future.

Completely agree	Agree	Undecided	Disagree	Completely disagree

54. Did you ever have to repeat a grade?

55. What career do you think is most important for the development of El Salvador?

   2. Classroom Teacher Survey

Section I: Educational Television (ETV)

(Questions 1-27 all have the same five alternatives: Completely agree, Agree, Undecided, Disagree, and Completely disagree.)

1. Students learn more with ETV than without.

2. It is more difficult to maintain classroom discipline when using ETV.

3. Classroom teachers improve their methods by watching the teleteacher.

4. ETV diminishes the importance of the classroom teacher.

5. ETV classes are an obstacle to the interpersonal relations between the classroom teacher and his students.

6. Students learn to study better by themselves when they receive their classes by ETV.

7. Classroom teachers learn to organize their schedules better with the ETV system.

8. There is a serious obstacle to learning by ETV because students cannot ask questions until the program has ended.

9. It is possible to teach more with ETV during the year, because ETV can cover more material.

10. Instruction by ETV makes the student more passive in class.

11. The ETV schedule does not allow enough flexibility for the classroom teacher to teach his material.

12. ETV helps parents become more interested in the education of their children.

13. Instruction by ETV gives information, but it cannot transmit values.

14. Students would learn more if they didn't have ETV.

Section II: Teaching and Education

15. Teaching is not a profession that gives much satisfaction.

16. All youngsters should have the opportunity to finish Third Cycle.

17. Increases in enrollment reduce the quality of secondary education.

18. The fundamental goal of education is to form the character of the child.

19. I would encourage my best students to become teachers.

20. Only the best students should continue studying after primary school.

21. In El Salvador, teachers are much respected.

22. The majority of Third Cycle students is not very interested in learning.

23. I would remain in education even if I found another job with a better salary.

24. Many students do not respect their teachers.

25. The most important goal of education is to develop reasoning.

26. The great majority of students is motivated to make good use of Third Cycle education.

27. The current Educational Reform is moving toward high quality Third Cycle education.

Section III: The Prestige of Occupations

28. Please indicate your idea of the prestige of each one of the following occupations (mark your answer with an "X" under: Very high, High, Average, Low, or Very low).

Bookkeeper	Accountant
Day-laborer	Architect
Engineer	Electrician
Small farmer	High school teacher
Brick-layer	Nurse
Doctor	Bilingual secretary
Industrial technician	Insurance agent
Chauffeur	Primary school teacher
Lawyer	Business manager
Soldier	

29. According to your personal experience, please indicate how you consider each of the following problems, marking an "X" under: Very serious, Serious, Minor, or Very minor.

Problems in the Classroom

A. Guides and workbooks don't arrive on time.
B. Lack of teaching materials.
C. Too many students in class.
D. Poverty of the students and their environment.
E. The behavior of students.
F. Technical problems in the reception of teleclasses.

Problems in the Educational System

G. Lack of supervision
H. Lack of parents' cooperation.
I. The economic situation of teachers.
J. School administration.
K. The efficiency of the Ministry of Education.
L. Lack of teachers with a "vocation" for teaching.
M. Changes in the system of evaluation and promotion.
N. Method of appointing teachers.

Section V: Personal Data

30. Birthplace: (City and Department)

Do you reside in the city where you teach?
If you answered "No" above, where is your permanent residence?

Age: Sex:

31. Mark in one of the following how long you have been teaching with ETV:

First year I've taught with ITV
Second year I've taught with ITV
I don't teach with ITV

32. Mark your classification as primary school teacher, if you have one, and for the other levels mark only those you have graduated from, except university.

Teacher classification:

Class B   Class A and High school
Class A   Class A and Accountant
High school   High school and Accountant
Accountant   Class A, High school, and
                 Accountant

Higher education:

No higher education
Superior Normal
1-2 years at the university
3 or more years at the university

33. Date when became a teacher:
    Date when became a secondary teacher:

34. Mark the subjects you teach:

Mathematics   Social studies   English
Natural science Spanish

3. The School and Community Survey

The School

A. Building

1. Rented ___   Owned by the government ___

2. Date of construction:

3. Construction material of the building:

4. Design as a school: poor   mediocre   good

5. Sufficient lighting (natural or electric):
   sufficient   insufficient   very insufficient

6. General condition of the building: poor   mediocre   good

B. Teaching Conditions

1. The noise from some classes or from physical education bothers other classes: rarely   sometimes   frequently

2. Sufficient teaching materials:

   sufficient   insufficient   very insufficient

3. Specific materials that are needed:

4. Quality of the teaching materials: poor   mediocre   good

C. Classrooms

1. Number of classrooms:

2. Taking into account the current number of students that use them, the size of the classrooms is:

   too big   too small   just right

D. Desks

1. Owned by the Ministry   Owned by the students
   Owned by the Patronato (local sponsoring group)

2. Are there enough? How many lacking?

E. Facilities

   __ Library for the teachers
   __ Library for the students
   __ Special room for the library
   __ Laboratory
   __ Bathrooms
   __ Recreation area
   __ Area for physical education
   __ Auditorium
   __ Mimeograph machine

F. Location

1. The climate bothers the classes:

	In the morning	In the afternoon
Rarely	__	__
Sometimes	__	__
Frequently	__	__
Very frequently	__	__

2. The noise from outside the school bothers the classes:

   rarely   sometimes   frequently   very frequently

G. Administration

1. __ Combined with an Institute (an Institute is a senior high school) in the same building
   __ Combined with a primary school in the same building
   __ Not combined with any other school

2. Number of Third Cycle students: ___

   In the morning: 7th ___   8th ___   9th ___
   In the afternoon: 7th ___   8th ___   9th ___

3. Number of teachers in the Third Cycle: ___

   How many teach both morning and afternoon? ___
   How many teachers short are you? ___
   How many have to teach a subject outside their specialty? ___

4. Number of classes in Third Cycle: ___

   In the morning: 7th ___   8th ___   9th ___
   In the afternoon: 7th ___   8th ___   9th ___

H. The School Director

1. __ Permanent position   __ Temporary appointment

2. Sex:

3. Experience: How many years of teaching experience? ___
                  How many years experience as a director? ___

4. Training: __ Graduate of Normal School
                __ Graduate of Bachillerato
                __ Graduate of the Superior Normal School

5. Retraining: __ A year at San Andres
                  __ Three summers at San Andres
                  __ One summer at San Andres
                  __ None

6. Residence: __ Lives permanently in the community
                 __ Lives in the community only during the week
                 __ Lives outside the community

7. What are the major problems the school has?

I. The Students

1. Where do the students come from?
___ All of them come from the city
___ The majority come from the city, others from the cantones*
___ The majority come from the cantones

2. Is the mix of students different in 7th grade than in 8th or 9th? In what way is it different?

3. Do you have problems with student conduct?
rarely   sometimes   frequently   very frequently

4. Have you had time to organize extracurricular activities this year? What kind? How often?

5. Have you had more activities in past years? If yes, why the change this year?

6. Do your 7th grade students come from one or from a number of primary schools?
___ All of them come from one primary
___ The majority come from one, but some come from other(s)
___ They come from a number, with: ___ equal preparation
                                   ___ different levels of preparation

7. Have you had meetings with the parents' group this year? How many times? For what reasons?

The Community

A. Available Education

1. Are there schools in the community where students can continue their education after Third Cycle?
___ Commercial courses   ___ Day   ___ Night
___ Bachillerato   ___ Day   ___ Night
___ No schools

2. If there are no such schools in the city, are there such schools in the area where students can commute every day?
___ Commercial schools   ___ Day   ___ Night
___ Bachillerato   ___ Day   ___ Night
___ No schools

3. What are the graduates of last year doing?
___ % have looked for work
___ % have looked for work and begun to go to night classes in: ___ the Bachillerato ___ the Commercial School
___ % are going to the bachillerato during the day
___ % are going to the canton corte during the day
___ % other

4. How easy is it for the graduates of Third Cycle to find work appropriate to the level of their education in this city?

	Men	Women
All can find work		
The majority can find work		
50% can find work		
The majority can't find work		
No one can find work		

B. Accessibility

1. How long does it take to go by bus to (Santa Ana, Sonsonate, San Miguel, San Salvador)?

2. How many buses a day come here?

3. How long does it take to go by bus to San Salvador?

4. How many buses go to San Salvador from here every day?

5. How far is it to the nearest paved highway?

C. Specific Data

1. Is there a bank here?

2. Is there a movie theater here?

3. What is the population?

4. How many private phones?

5. How many registered vehicles?

6. What is the percentage of paved streets in the city?

7. How many newspapers sold?

4. Classroom Teachers' Feedback Survey

INSTRUCTIONS:

The following material refers only to the Math course at the grade level indicated. Please consider only this course when giving your answers.

For each of the following questions you should respond in the following manner:

If the statement is: "The ability of most students to learn Mathematics"

1   2   3   4   5

you should decide whether you think that ability is high or low. If you think it is very high, you should make a circle around the number "5". If you think it is very low, you should make the circle around the number "1". If the ability is mid-way between high and low, "3" would be the appropriate number to circle. If it is high, but not very high, you should circle the number "4". If it is low, but not very low, you should circle the number "2".

Learning

1. What students learn from mathematics with ETV.

2. What students learned from mathematics before the introduction of ETV.

Motivation

3. The motivation of the students in mathematics since the introduction of ETV.

4. The motivation of students in mathematics before the introduction of ETV.

Guides for Teachers of Mathematics

5. The aid to teaching given by the guides of mathematics.

6. The practical value of classroom activities suggested by the guides for mathematics.

7. The relationship between the guides of mathematics and the tele-classes of mathematics.

The Teleteacher of Mathematics

8. The teleteacher's knowledge of mathematics.

9. The teleteacher's ability to teach mathematics.

10. The teleteacher's ability to make students participate.

11. The teleteacher's ability to teach mathematics, in comparison with the majority of classroom teachers:

| Much less | Less | Equal | Much more | More |

Student Workbooks for Mathematics

12. The number of exercises generally included in the workbooks:

| Very insufficient | A bit insufficient | Adequate | A bit excessive | Very excessive |

Teleclasses for Mathematics

13. In general, the content of the teleclasses?

14. The quantity of exposition by the teleteacher?

15. The quantity of audiovisual materials (movies and slides) used in the teleclasses?

16. The legibility of graphics (drawings, signs, etc.) used in the teleclasses?

17. What the audiovisual materials (movies and slides) contribute to the effectiveness of teleclasses?

Teaching

18. The help that ITV could provide (at its maximum) in the teaching of mathematics.

19. The help that ITV, since its introduction, has given in the teaching of mathematics.

5. TEACHER OBSERVATION FORM*

SCHOOL _____	TOWN _____
TEACHER _____	SCIENCE / / HUMANITIES / /
GRADE _____	TV / / NO TV / / ACT / / WB / /
SUBJECT _____	The teacher had prepared his class
THEME OF THE LESSON _____	in advance: / / Yes / / No
DATE _____	

The observation form was built on a time basis. As seen below, each activity is a series of boxes:

1. Lectures   / 1 / 2 / 3 / 4 / 5 /

Each individual box (/ /) represents five minutes of class time. During the first five minute observation period, the observer marked the first box of every activity engaged in by both teacher and students. For example, let us suppose that during the first five minutes observed the teacher began by lecturing for three minutes on a new math formula. He then asked a student where the chalk was, spent a minute writing problems concerning the new formula on the board, and afterwards directed students to solve the problems in their notebooks. For those five minutes, the observer would have marked the following items in this way:

TEACHER:

1. Lectures   ▦ / / / / /
4. Asks procedure questions   / 1 / / / /
9. Uses blackboard   / / ▦ / / /

STUDENTS:

8. Work individually   / / / ▦ / /

T E A C H E R

1. Lectures   ///////////////////////
2. Dictates   ///////////////////////
3. Explains (responding to Spanish question)   / / / / /
4. Asks procedure questions   / / / / /
5. Asks memory questions to group   / / / / /
6. Asks memory questions to individuals   / / / / /
7. Asks opinion questions   / / / / /
8. Asks thought questions   / / / / /
9. Uses blackboard   ///////////////////////
10. Uses demonstrations   ///////////////////////
11. Uses audio-visual materials   ///////////////////////
12. Directs exercises in groups   ///////////////////////
13. Works individually with students   ///////////////////////
14. Supervises student activity   ///////////////////////
15. Suggests individual projects   ///////////////////////
16. Reviews individual projects   ///////////////////////
17. Assigns homework   ///////////////////////

For those activities requiring an accurate time measure (lectures, uses blackboard, etc.), each five minute box was subdivided into one minute segments. In cases where frequency was more important than duration (asks procedure questions, etc.), the observer marked each separate occurrence.

* Administered in 1970

18. Assigns investigations as homework ///////////////////////////

19. Checks homework ///////////////////////////

20. Teacher behavior during Teleclass: _____

21. Student behavior during Teleclass: _____

S T U D E N T S

1. Ask procedure questions / / / / / /

2. Ask memory questions / / / / / /

3. Ask thought questions / / / / / /

4. Go to blackboard ///////////////////////////

5. Give opinions / / / / / /

6. Take part in discussions ///////////////////////////

7. Work in small groups ///////////////////////////

8. Work individually ///////////////////////////

9. Work on individual projects (chosen by students) ///////////////////////////

10. Repetition drill ///////////////////////////

11. Question-answer drills ///////////////////////////

12. Dramatizations ///////////////////////////

Supplementary Data

TABLE D.1

General Ability and Reading Intercorrelations

Samples and tests	Correlation	Variance accounted for	Residual variance
Cohort A:			
Gen. abil. beg. 7th X gen. abil. end 9th	.743[a]	55%	45%
Reading beg. 7th X reading beg. 9th	.870	76	24
Cohort B:			
Gen. abil. beg. 7th X gen. abil. end 9th	.885	78	22
Reading beg. 7th X reading end 9th	.776	60	40
Cohort C:			
Gen. abil. beg. 7th X gen. abil. end 8th	.813	66	34
Reading beg. 7th X reading end 8th	.802	64	36

[a]Corrected for unreliability; see Appendix B.

TABLE D.2

Correlations: Basic Skills by Background Variables

Variable	General ability (beg. 7th)			Reading (beg. 7th)		
	Cohort A	Cohort B	Cohort C	Cohort A	Cohort B	Cohort C
Sex (female = 0; male = 1)	.140	.124	.151	.209	.151	.131
Age	-.274	-.376	-.319	-.223	-.324	-.280
Father's ed.	.157	.321	.227	.141	.333	.255
Mother's ed.	.145	.298	.209	.107	.299	.235
Wealth	.171	.283	.203	.127	.464	.253
Urbanization (rural = 1; urban - 5)	.232	.301	.331	.226	.252	.378

NOTE: All correlations are significant at $p < .001$. For Cohorts A and B disattenuated coefficients (corrected for unreliability) are reported. The relevant measurement models are fully explained in Appendix B.

TABLE D.3

ITV and Non-ITV Scores in General Ability and Reading

Test	Cohort A[a] (enter 1969)		Cohort B (enter 1970)		Cohort C (enter 1971)	
	ITV (N=419)	Trad. (N=156)	ITV (N=318)	Reform only (N=204)	ITV (N=343)	Reform only (N=130)
Gen. ability						
Beg. 7th	86.99	88.56	57.93	54.69	51.62	49.70
Beg. 8th	74.61	74.32	70.70	65.81		
End 8th					65.23	59.95
End 9th	87.80	86.31	82.56	75.44		
Reading						
Beg. 7th	63.32	64.79	37.96	34.16	32.25	30.01
Beg. 8th	48.03	48.45	46.67	42.53		
End 8th					42.93	41.70
Beg. 9th	51.76	55.60				
End 9th			56.04	50.91		

NOTE: The small or negative gains reported for Cohort A reflect the change from an easier test in grade 7 to a more difficult one in grades 8 and 9. For Cohorts B and C, schools located in San Salvador were excluded from the calculations, since all of these had ITV.

[a]In Cohort A only, the sample sizes for the reading test differed from those for general ability: in classes with Reform and ITV, N=468; in Traditional classes, N=160.

TABLE D.4

General Ability and Reading Score Changes, by Instructional Condition
(excluding schools in San Salvador)

Test and Group	Gain		Residual gain	
	ITV	No ITV	ITV	No ITV
General ability				
Cohort A	.811	-2.250[a]	.947[a]	-2.588[a]
Cohort B	24.623[b]	20.750[a]	24.361[a]	21.690[a]
Cohort C	13.606[a]	10.254[a]	13.522[a]	10.405[a]
Reading				
Cohort A	-11.556	-9.188	-11.433	-9.563
Cohort B	18.085	16.750	17.969	17.152
Cohort C	10.676	11.692	10.711	11.625

[a]Difference between ITV and No ITV significant at p < .05.

TABLE D.5

Overall Means, Gains, and Percentage Gains in Math Scores

Tests and gains	Cohort A (N=712)	Cohort B (N=505)	Cohort C (N=558)
Begin 7th	12.087[a]	15.315[b]	14.125[b]
End 7th	17.896	18.633	17.439
Gain	5.809	3.318	3.314
Percent gain	48.1%	21.7%	23.5%
Begin 8th	15.995[b]	13.658[b]	16.631[c]
End 8th	17.949	16.179	19.443
Gain	1.954	2.521	2.812
Percent gain	12.0%	18.5%	16.9%
Begin 9th	15.476[b]	18.197[c]	
End 9th	18.021	22.929	
Gain	2.545	4.732	
Percent gain	16.4%	26.0%	

[a]Number of correct answers on 50-item test, 1969 version.

[b]Number of correct answers on 50-item test, 1970-71 version.

[c]Number of correct answers on 60-item test, 1972 version.

TABLE D.6

Overall Means, Gains, and Percentage Gains in Science Scores

Tests and gains	Cohort A (N=705)	Cohort B (N=519)	Cohort C (N=573)
Begin 7th	18.368[a]	20.784[b]	19.402[b]
End 7th	23.921	25.493	23.452
Gain	5.553	4.709	4.05
Percent gain	30.2%	22.7%	20.9%
Begin 8th	24.193[b]	21.979[b]	22.127[c]
End 8th	25.983	24.688	22.285
Gain	1.790	2.709	.158
Percent gain	7.4%	12.3%	.7%
Begin 9th	20.538[b]	25.364[c]	
End 9th	22.571	28.552	
Gain	2.033	3.188	
Percent gain	9.9%	12.6%	

[a]Number of correct answers on 50-item test, 1969 version.
[b]Number of correct answers on 50-item test, 1970-71 version.
[c]Number of correct answers on 60-item test, 1972 version.

TABLE D.7

Overall Means, Gains, and Percentage Gains in Social Studies Score

Tests and gains	Cohort A (N=706)	Cohort B (N=519)	Cohort C (N=562)
Begin 7th	26.973[a]	24.194[b]	21.752[b]
End 7th	34.207	30.869	27.373
Gain	7.234	6.675	5.621
Percent gain	26.8%	27.6%	25.8%
Begin 8th	24.642[b]	23.085[b]	23.289[c]
End 8th	27.152	25.951	27.979
Gain	2.510	2.866	4.690
Percent gain	10.2%	12.4%	20.1%
Begin 9th	20.035[b]	25.311[c]	
End 9th	21.750	26.373	
Gain	1.715	1.062	
Percent gain	8.6%	4.2%	

[a]Number of correct answers on 50-item test, 1969 version.
[b]Number of correct answers on 50-item test, 1970-71 version.
[c]Number of correct answers on 60-item test, 1972 version.

TABLE D.8

Math Achievement Scores

Tests and gains	Cohort A		Cohort B		Cohort C	
	ITV (N=537)[a]	Trad. (N=175)	ITV (N=413)	Reform, No ITV (N=90)	ITV (N=434)	Reform, No ITV (N=124)
Begin 7th	11.971	12.444	15.334	15.266	14.233	13.746
End 7th	18.236	16.853	19.019	16.862	17.297	17.935
Gain	6.265	4.409	3.685	1.596	3.064	4.189
Percent gain	52.3%	35.4%	24.0%	10.5%	21.5%	30.5%
Begin 8th	16.130	15.580	13.814	12.943	16.652	16.560
End 8th	18.330	16.780	16.019	16.911	19.899	17.847
Gain	2.200	1.200	2.205	3.968	3.247	1.287
Percent gain	13.6%	7.7%	16.0%	30.7%	19.5%	7.8%
Begin 9th	15.510	15.370	18.442	17.073		
End 9th	18.660	16.060	23.386	20.832		
Gain	3.150	.690	4.944	3.759		
Percent gain	20.3%	4.5%	26.8%	22.0%		

[a] All sample figures are minimum N.

TABLE D.9

Science Achievement Scores

Tests and gains	Cohort A		Cohort B		Cohort C	
	ITV (N=527)	Trad. (N=178)	ITV (N=425)	Reform, No ITV (N=94)	ITV (N=444)	Reform, No ITV (N=129)
Begin 7th	18.059	19.282	20.720	21.074	19.474	19.154
End 7th	24.768	21.412	25.974	23.319	23.698	22.605
Gain	6.709	2.130	5.254	2.245	4.224	3.451
Percent gain	37.2%	11.0%	25.4%	10.6%	21.7%	18.0%
Begin 8th	25.195	21.225	22.410	20.028	22.518	20.783
End 8th	26.794	23.581	24.971	23.408	22.592	21.227
Gain	1.599	2.356	2.561	3.380	.074	.437
Percent gain	6.3%	11.1%	11.4%	16.9%	.3%	2.1%
Begin 9th	21.372	18.068	25.921	22.850		
End 9th	23.385	20.162	28.697	27.897		
Gain	2.013	2.094	2.776	5.047		
Percent gain	9.4%	11.6%	10.7%	22.1%		

TABLE D.10

Social Studies Achievement Scores

| Tests and gains | Cohort A | | Cohort B | | Cohort C | |
	ITV (N=527)	Trad. (N=179)	ITV (N=425)	Reform, No ITV (N=94)	ITV (N=439)	Reform, No ITV (N=123)
Begin 7th	26.627	27.990	24.308	23.681	22.228	20.054
End 7th	35.557	30.232	31.715	27.043	28.330	23.959
Gain	8.930	2.242	7.407	3.362	6.102	3.905
Percent gain	33.5%	8.0%	30.5%	14.2%	27.5%	19.5%
Begin 8th	26.180	20.112	23.836	19.689	23.567	22.298
End 8th	28.924	22.229	26.419	23.837	28.622	25.682
Gain	2.744	2.117	2.583	4.148	5.055	3.384
Percent gain	10.5%	10.5%	10.8%	21.1%	21.4%	15.2%
Begin 9th	20.524	18.594	25.605	23.981		
End 9th	21.748	21.754	26.741	24.710		
Gain	1.224	3.160	1.136	.729		
Percent gain	6.0%	17.0%	4.4%	3.0%		

TABLE D.11

Correlations Between Cognitive Skills and Background Variables
(29 classrooms)

Variable							Variable							
	1	2	3	4	5	6	7	8	9	10	11	12	13	14
Personal and family														
1. Father's ed.														
2. Mother's ed.	.822													
3. Age	-.728	-.726												
4. Percent repeaters	-.633	-.644	.613											
5. Wealth	.715	.729	-.792	-.363										
School variables														
6. School size	.644	.488	-.724	-.538	.629									
7. Physical condition	.311	.364	-.584	-.257	.480	.475								
8. Teaching materials	.360	.367	-.309	-.447	.267	.183	.427							
9. School facilities	.393	.300	-.301	-.531	.168	.586	.254	.549						
Community variables														
10. Educational availability	.609	.499	-.633	-.385	.520	.708	.327	.111	.330					
11. Access to city	.443	.392	-.333	-.340	.530	.351	.474	.499	.220	.242				
12. Community resources	.773	.603	-.704	-.450	.739	.792	.407	.347	.355	.844	.530			
Cognitive skills														
13. Begin 7th	.771	.694	-.580	-.441	.711	.434	.403	.262	.163	.397	.502	.577		
14. Begin 8th	.666	.584	-.626	-.418	.625	.505	.632	.323	.296	.469	.592	.587	.741	
15. End 9th	.563	.624	-.683	-.436	.649	.454	.624	.336	.215	.304	.479	.477	.733	.803

NOTE: Correlations larger than .31 were significant at $p < .05$.

TABLE D.12

Correlations of Predictor Variables, ITV, and Cognitive Index Scores
(26 schools outside San Salvador)

Variable	Cognitive index beg. 7th	Cognitive index end 9th	Cognitive index change 7th to 9th
Father's education	.75	.41	-.41
Wealth	.64	.57	-.13
Age	-.47	-.63	-.12
Repeated grade (0=No, 1=Yes)	-.32	-.31	.04
Community resources	.49	.36	-.18
School size	.34	.38	.01
Adequacy of teaching materials	.03	.09	.06
Educational opportunity	.32	.20	-.15
Access to city	.30	.24	-.09
Physical condition of school	.14	.43	.28
ITV (0=No, 1=Yes)	.07	.52	.45

TABLE D.13

Correlation of Student Attitudes with Control Variables:
ITV Subsample, Cohort B (N=400)

Attitude	Father's ed.	Wealth	Age	Sex	Urbanization	Gen. Abil. (March '70)
Learn more with ITV						
(10/70)	-.02	-.02	.07	-.01	.16	-.01
(10/71)	-.06	-.10	.09	-.03	.13	-.04
ITV more difficult						
(10/70)	-.06	-.01	.09	.05	-.04	-.16
(10/71)	-.03	.03	-.05	.08	-.12	-.09
See ITV clearly						
(10/70)	-.02	-.10	.08	-.06	.18	-.09
(10/71)	-.05	-.11	.16	-.11	.12	-.09
Teacher prefers ITV						
(10/70)	.09	-.04	.04	.06	.15	-.03
(10/71)	-.00	.02	.03	-.04	.08	-.02

TABLE D.14

Correlation of Student Attitudes Toward Individual Teleseries
with Control Variables, Cohort B (N=400)

Attitude	Father's ed.	Wealth	Age	Sex	Urbanization	Gen. Abil. (March '70)
Math						
(3/71)	-.15	-.17	.16	-.07	.15	-.15
(10/71)	-.06	-.09	.12	-.01	.16	-.07
(10/72)	-.10	-.09	.10	.05	.08	-.06
Science						
(3/71)	-.06	-.05	.05	-.08	-.01	.02
(10/71)	-.00	-.00	.08	-.01	.04	-.03
(10/72)	-.04	-.02	.00	.03	-.06	-.05
Social Studies						
(3/71)	-.13	-.12	.13	-.04	.09	-.15
(10/71)	-.07	-.05	.04	.02	.10	-.09
(10/72)	-.13	-.07	.10	.02	.08	-.17
English						
(3/71)	-.08	-.09	.04	-.14	.18	.02
(10/71)	-.13	-.09	.10	-.06	.18	-.05
(10/72)	-.17	-.09	.06	-.22	.13	-.04
Spanish						
(3/71)	-.08	-.14	.13	-.10	.15	-.14
(10/71)	.03	-.04	.09	-.09	.09	-.04
(10/72)	-.12	-.12	.12	-.12	.08	-.14

TABLE D.15

Educational Aspirations, by Sex

Time	Finish Third Cycle only		Finish all secondary		University or post-grad	
	Boys	Girls	Boys	Girls	Boys	Girls
Cohort A (N=902)						
Begin 7th	12.7%	7.1%	43.5%	65.1%	42.8%	26.9%
End 8th	5.9	3.9	45.7	57.0	48.4	39.2
End 9th	2.8	1.6	34.3	52.6	62.8	45.8
Cohort B (N=707)						
Begin 7th	11.5	5.5	49.9	56.6	38.4	38.0
End 8th	5.2	1.4	32.9	44.7	61.9	53.8
End 9th	2.3	1.3	40.9	48.9	56.7	49.8
Cohort C (N=600)						
Begin 7th	13.1	5.5	42.9	49.6	44.0	44.9
End 8th	8.9	4.0	40.5	56.1	50.6	39.9

TABLE D.16

Occupational Choice Levels, by Sex

Time	Level one		Level two		Level three	
	Boys	Girls	Boys	Girls	Boys	Girls
Cohort A (N=902)						
Begin 7th	6.7%	0.9%	58.5%	83.0%	34.4%	16.0%
End 9th	3.1	0.3	45.4	64.2	51.5	35.5
Cohort B (N=707)						
Begin 7th	3.6	0.0	52.9	74.5	43.8	24.1
End 9th	4.4	1.4	49.4	64.1	46.2	34.5
Cohort C (N=600)						
Begin 7th	6.2	0.0	52.5	83.1	41.3	16.9
End 8th	3.1	1.2	50.7	69.1	44.4	27.2

Published Reports on El Salvador's Educational Reform

All reports prepared and published by the Institute for Communication Research, Stanford University, Stanford, California, on behalf of the Academy for Educational Development, under Contract with the United States Agency for International Development. Reports marked* are out of print.

1. First meeting of the Advisory Committee. Administrative Rept. No. 1, October 1968.*
2. Design of the study. Research Rept. No. 1, December 1968.*
3. The use of television in the El Salvador program of educational reform: Differences between this project and some others. Administrative Rept. No. 2, April 1969.
4. The El Salvador educational reform: Some effects of the first teacher retraining course. Research Rept. No. 2, July 1969 (Emile G. McAnany, Generoso Gil, Jr., Donald F. Roberts).*
5. Measuring educational development through classroom interaction. Research Memo No. 1, September 1969 (Wilbur Schramm).*
6. Parents talk about ETV in El Salvador. Research Memo No. 2, October 1969 (Luis F. Valero Iglesias, Emile G. McAnany).*
7. Feedback for instructional television. Research Memo No. 3, December 1969 (Wilbur Schramm).
8. Research and evaluation in the El Salvador project of educational reform: What is being tested and why. Research Memo No. 4, January 1970.*
9. Television and educational reform in El Salvador: Summary report of the first year of research. Research Rept. No. 3, May 1970 (Wilbur Schramm, Emile G. McAnany, John K. Mayo, Robert C. Hornik).
10. Television and educational reform in El Salvador: Complete report on the first year of research. Research Rept. No. 4, July 1970 (Emile G. McAnany, Robert C. Hornik, John K. Mayo).
11. Teacher observation in El Salvador. Research Rept. No. 5, January 1971 (Judith A. Mayo).

12. Feedback on student learning for instructional television in El Salvador. Research Rept. No. 6, February 1971 (Ana Merino de Manzano, Robert C. Hornik, John K. Mayo).

13. Television and educational reform in El Salvador: Complete report on the second year of research. Research Rept. No. 7, March 1971 (Wilbur Schramm, John K. Mayo, Emile G. McAnany, Robert C. Hornik).

14. An administrative history of El Salvador's educational reform. Research Rept. No. 8, November 1971 (John K. Mayo, Judith A. Mayo).

15. Instructional television in national educational reform. Research Rept. No. 9, March 1973 (Wilbur Schramm).

16. Television and educational reform in El Salvador: Report on the third year of research. Research Rept. No. 10, March 1972 (Robert C. Hornik, Henry Ingle, John K. Mayo, Judith A. Mayo, Emile G. McAnany, Wilbur Schramm).

17. Television and educational reform in El Salvador: Report on the fourth year of research. Research Rept. No. 11, May 1973 (Henry Ingle, Yolanda Ingle, Robert C. Hornik, John K. Mayo, Emile G. McAnany, Wilbur Schramm).

18. Television and educational reform in El Salvador: Follow-up study on the first group of ninth grade graduates. Research Rept. No. 12, June 1973 (Henry Ingle, in cooperation with Jose Velasco and Victor Zelada).

19. Television and educational reform in El Salvador: Final report. August 1973 (Robert C. Hornik, Henry T. Ingle, John K. Mayo, Emile G. McAnany, Wilbur Schramm).

Index

Ability, general
—gains in: and scores at beginning of
7th grade, 57, 67; and background
variables, 66-68; effect of ITV on,
68-69, 82; by classroom units, 77-81;
compared to reading gains, 84
—testing of, 176-77; in evaluating ITV,
56-64 *passim*; in determining skills
index of classrooms, 79-80; techniques for, 176-77
Abstractions, and ITV, 92-93
Academic background as criterion in
ITV staff selection, 34, 37
Accounting, as a career, 104, 120
Achievement: tests of, in teleteacher
selection, 34; with ITV, 56-85; gains
in, 72-73, 82, 84; scores, and cognitive skills index, 79-80; and attitudes
of student toward subject or teleseries, 91-98 *passim*. *See also*
Learning
Acoustics, classroom, 49
Administration: of Ministry of Education, pre-Reform, 21-22; overall, of
ITV, 27, 28-29; of ITV production,
30-31, 38-39, 40; of schools with ITV,
51; problems of, and validity of data,
58n, 59; teachers' assessment of, 129,
135; and strength of leadership,
165-66, 167
Advisers: role of foreigners, 27, 33, 37,
52-54, 166-67; classroom supervisors
as, 48-49, 51f; cost-effectiveness of,
53
Adult education, 169, 175
Affluence, community, 79f. *See also*
Socioeconomic position

Age: school-starting, 20; and attitude
toward ITV, 95; target, for Reform,
27, 169; of three cohorts, 61; and
urbanization, 62; and scores at
beginning of 7th grade, 65f, 77, 79,
179; and gains in scores, 66-67, 70,
77, 180, 181-82; effect of Reform on
disparities due to, 82, 85; and
aspiration level, 105f
Agency for International Development,
see USAID
Agriculture, 7-17 *passim*, 21
American Samoa, ITV in, 33
ANDES (Asociacíon Nacional de
Educadores Salvadoreños), 127
Annualization of costs, 150n
Aspirations, educational and occupational: of students, 100-111, 116-19;
changes in over time, 101-4 *passim*;
sex differences in, 104; origins of,
105-8; and parental attitudes, 108-9;
of parents for sons, 111-15, 119;
and parental aspirations, 112, 114f,
119; validity of, 116f; effect of Reform on, 118, 164; consistency of,
119; reality of, 121
Assignment of teachers, 2, 65, 129, 135
Assistance, foreign, *see* Advisers;
Grants; Loans
Attitude, 6; as problem for ITV
production, 32
Attitudes
—of parents: and student aspirations,
108-9; toward ITV, 110-11
—of students: toward school and ITV,
86-99, 139, 141; toward individual
teleseries, 91-93; toward individual